EVENTS THAT CHANGED THE WORLD

1840–1860

=The Nineteenth Century=

Jodie L. Zdrok, *Book Editor*

Bruce Glassman, *Vice president*
Bonnie Szumski, *Publisher*
Helen Cothran, *Managing Editor*

GREENHAVEN PRESS
An imprint of Thomson Gale, a part of The Thomson Corporation

THOMSON

™

GALE

Detroit • New York • San Francisco • San Diego • New Haven, Conn.
Waterville, Maine • London • Munich

Thomson and Star Logo are trademarks and Gale and Greenhaven Press are registered trademarks used herein under license.

For more information, contact
Greenhaven Press
27500 Drake Rd.
Farmington Hills, MI 48331-3535
Or you can visit our Internet site at http://www.gale.com

Cover credit: AKG-images/Archives CDA
Library of Congress, 30, 148, 159

LIBRARY OF CONGRESS CATALOGING-IN-PUBLICATION DATA

1840–1860 / Jodie L. Zdrok, book editor.
  p. cm. — (Events that changed the world)
Includes bibliographical references and index.
ISBN 0-7377-2033-6 (lib. bdg. : alk. paper)
  1. History, Modern—19th century. I. Zdrok, Jodie L. II. Series.
D358.A126 2005
909.81—dc22
                                  2004042513

Printed in the United States of America

CONTENTS

message, captures Morse's own enthusiasm and sense of awe about his success.

Event 3: The Irish Potato Famine: June 1845

Event 4: Ether Is Demonstrated as a Surgical Anesthetic: October 16, 1846

Event 5: The *Communist Manifesto* Is Published: January 1848

of achieving a classless society in which private property will be abolished.

Event 6: Revolution Sweeps Europe: February 22, 1848

1. The Revolutions of 1848 Changed European Politics

Event 7: The U.S.-Mexican War Ends: May 30, 1848

1. Polk Waged an Unjust War of Aggression

2. Mexican Landowners Were Treated Unfairly

Event 8: The First U.S. Woman's Rights Convention Convenes: July 19–20, 1848

1. Courage and Vision Launched the Women's Movement

Event 11: Commodore Perry "Opens" Japan: July 14, 1853

1. The United States Reaches Across the Pacific

Westward expansion influenced the American mission to Japan, but Commodore Perry's reception upon the expedition's return was tempered by domestic concerns.

2. Perry Meets the Japanese Delegates

The meeting with Japan's Imperial delegation was a ceremonious, friendly affair.

Event 12: The Crimean War Begins: March 28, 1854

1. The Crimean War Brought Change and Innovation

The war helped push a politically unstable Europe into an era of reform. It also launched a number of innovations.

Event 13: Florence Nightingale Serves in the Crimean War: November 1854

1. The Founder of Modern Nursing

One of nineteenth-century England's most influential women, Florence Nightingale founded modern nursing and was a recognized authority on public health and hospital management.

Event 14: Darwin Presents the Theory of Evolution: November 24, 1859

FOREWORD

I n 1543 a Polish astronomer named Nicolaus Copernicus published a book entitled *De revolutionibus orbium coelestium* in which he theorized that Earth revolved around the Sun. In 1688, during the Glorious Revolution, Dutch prince William of Orange invaded England and overthrew King James II. In 1922 Irish author James Joyce's novel *Ulysses*, which describes one day in Dublin, was published.

Although these events are seemingly unrelated, occurring in different nations and in different centuries, they all share the distinction of having changed the world. Although Copernicus's book had a relatively minor impact at the time of its publication, it eventually had a momentous influence. The Copernican system provided a foundation on which future scientists could develop an accurate understanding of the solar system. Perhaps more importantly, it required humanity to contemplate the possibility that Earth, far from occupying a special place at the center of creation, was merely one planet in a vast universe. In doing so, it forced a reevaluation of the Christian cosmology that had served as the foundation of Western culture. As professor Thomas S. Kuhn writes, "The drama of Christian life and the morality that had been made dependent upon it would not readily adapt to a universe in which the earth was just one of a number of planets."

Like the Copernican revolution, the Glorious Revolution of 1688–1689 had a profound influence on the future of Western societies. By deposing James II, William and his wife, Mary, ended the Stuart dynasty, a series of monarchs who had favored the Catholic Church and had limited the power of Parliament for decades. Under William and Mary, Parliament passed the Bill of Rights, which established the legislative supremacy of Parliament and barred Roman Catholics from the throne. These actions initiated the gradual process by which the power of the government of England shifted from the monarchy to Parliament, establishing a democratic system that would be copied, with some variations, by the United States and other democratic societies worldwide.

Whereas the Glorious Revolution had a major impact in the political sphere, the publication of Joyce's novel *Ulysses* represented a revolution in literature. In an effort to capture the sense of chaos and discontinuity that permeated the culture in the wake of World War I, Joyce did away with the use of straightforward narrative that had dominated fiction up to that time. The novel, whose structure mirrors that of Homer's *Odyssey*, combines realistic descriptions of events with passages that convey the characters' inner experience by means of a technique known as stream of consciousness, in which the characters' thoughts and feelings are presented without regard to logic or narrative order. Due to its departure from the traditional modes of fiction, *Ulysses* is often described as one of the seminal works of modernist literature. As stated by Pennsylvania State University professor Michael H. Begnal, "*Ulysses* is the novel that changed the direction of 20th-century fiction written in English."

Copernicus's theory of a sun-centered solar system, the Glorious Revolution, and James Joyce's *Ulysses* are just three examples of time-bound events that have had far-reaching effects—for better or worse—on the progress of human societies worldwide. History is made up of an inexhaustible list of such events. In the twentieth century alone, for example, one can isolate any number of world-shattering moments: the first performance of Igor Stravinsky's ballet *The Rites of Spring* in 1913; Japan's attack on Pearl Harbor on December 7, 1941; the launch of the satellite *Sputnik* on October 4, 1957. These events variously influenced the culture, society, and political configuration of the twentieth century.

Greenhaven Press's Events That Changed the World series is designed to help readers learn about world history by examining seemingly random events that have had the greatest influence on the development of cultures, societies, and governments throughout the ages. The series is divided into sets of several anthologies, with each set covering a period of one hundred years. Each volume begins with an introduction that provides essential context on the time period being covered. Then, the major events of the era are covered by means of primary and secondary sources. Primary sources include firsthand accounts, speeches, correspondence, and other materials that bring history alive. Secondary sources analyze the profound effects the events had on the world. Each reading is preceded by an introduction that puts it in context and emphasizes the event's importance in the ongoing evolution of world history. Additional features add to the value of the series: An annotated table of contents and an index allow readers to quickly locate material of interest. A chronology provides an easy reference for contextual information. And a bibliography offers opportunities for further exploration. All of these features help to make the Events That Changed the World series a valuable resource for readers interested in the major events that have shaped the course of humanity.

The early nineteenth century was marked by political upheaval: the splintering of the European empire of Napoléon, the rise of anticolonial and nationalist movements, rebellion and wars of independence around the world between 1820 and 1840. Upheaval continued in the mid–nineteenth century, but between 1840 and 1860 the most radical change was social and economic rather than political.

Some of the social transformation of this period was the result of individual achievement and invention that was essentially unconnected. In May 1844 American inventor Samuel F.B. Morse tapped the first telegraph message, "What hath God wrought?"and ushered in a new era in communications; within a decade every state east of the Mississippi was linked by telegraph. American Quakers Lucretia Mott and Elizabeth Cady Stanton organized the Seneca Falls Convention of 1848 and galvanized the woman's rights movement. In the 1850s Florence Nightingale pioneered nursing methods in the Crimean War and hospital reform in Britain, improvements adopted by health-care systems worldwide. British naturalist Charles Darwin revolutionized the biological sciences with his theory of evolution, published in *On the Origin of Species* in 1859.

Many of the most significant events of the era, however, were not isolated achievements but clearly connected developments, characterized more by mass movements and pursuits than by individual accomplishment. This pivotal chain of events had profound effects in a very short time: In only twenty years, a crop failure in Ireland, the discovery of a gold nugget in California, and the debate over slavery combined to hasten the Civil War, lead to one of the largest immigration waves to the United States in its history, and change the way Americans viewed their destiny.

The Irish Potato Famine Spurs Immigration

A major link in the chain of events was a huge influx of European immigrants to the United States beginning in the mid-1840s. The largest group was Irish. For nearly two hundred years, Ireland's farm-based population had subsisted almost entirely on a single crop, potatoes, for both food and income. When a devastating fungus began rotting the potato crops in the fields in 1845, there was no surplus and no money to buy food elsewhere. Over the next five years nearly 1 million of Ireland's 8 million people died of starvation or disease. By 1854 the Irish potato famine had impelled nearly 2 million others to leave the country and settle in the United States, where most turned to factory work in increasingly congested eastern cities.

The Irish were joined by nearly a million Germans and French, refugees from the European revolutions of 1848; Swedes seeking relief from economic depression and in response to relaxation of emigration controls at home in the 1850s; and skilled industrial workers from Britain. German and Swedish farming communities spread in Wisconsin and Minnesota; British labor boosted the productivity of New England textile mills.

At first the new immigrants were tolerated if not welcomed, especially those groups who were most closely related to the English-speaking Protestant majority. As immigration increased, however, so did tensions between the native majority and Irish and German Catholics and non–English speakers, exacerbated by bad conditions in the urban slums where many immigrants lived.

Manifest Destiny Supports Westward Migration

The census of 1840 put the U.S. population at less than 17 million, sparse from today's perspective; at the time, however, there was a claustrophobic sense that the country was filling up fast. The addition of 4 million immigrants by 1860 intensified that alarm. America had entered the 1840s in an economic depression. Land in the East was not as cheap as it used to be. The solution for many seeking self-advancement: Go west.

Territorial expansion was the next link in the chain of events, driven not only by crowding in the East but also by widespread religious revival in the early 1840s. Few at the time doubted that God favored America; naturally, many argued, God wanted America to grow. This rationale contributed to the creation and popularity of the concept of manifest destiny, the belief in a mission, which some held was divinely ordained, to occupy all areas of the continent that did not yet belong to the United States and to extend American ideals and democratic institutions over peoples considered incapable of self-government, such as Native Americans.

The drive to the West was on. One 1843 wagon train, known as the Great Migration, alone comprised a thousand people and five thousand livestock. Until 1848, Oregon was the West Coast destination of choice. People who wanted to hide from family and business troubles, people without prospects, people driven simply by desire to own land could start again there if they managed to survive the six-month journey over the hazardous Oregon Trail. It was essentially a one-way trip; no one in the East expected the return of those who left. The trail to California, an even wilder place visited by few other than trappers and Mexican missionaries, was far less traveled.

The Gold Rush

All that changed in March 1848, when a San Francisco newspaper reported the discovery of gold on the American River near Sacramento. Soon reports of similar discoveries in the area reached the wider world, along with scientific estimations that, while the average concentration of gold in the earth's crust was five parts per billion, in California's Sierra region, gold occurred in concentrations as high as 100 million parts per billion. The next link in the era's chain of great events, the California gold rush, dominated transcontinental migration for the next fifteen years.

A quarter-million people looking west for opportunity shifted direction and descended on California with dreams of striking it rich. They not only crossed the Great Plains and Rocky Mountains by wagon train but sailed around Cape Horn and across the Pacific and trekked over the isthmus of Panama to get there. Chileans, Chinese, Australians, and French joined Native Americans, Mexicans, and American pioneers in a frenzy of prospecting and haphazard settlement.

The New American Dream and the Fast Track to California Statehood

Overnight, it seemed, Americans' traditional Puritan ethic of gradual accumulation of worldly goods through hard work gave way to what historian H.W. Brands characterizes as the new American dream of instant wealth achieved with audacity and good luck. Indeed, the California gold rush proved that things could happen fast: Fortunes were made and lost. Cities sprang up in response to sudden demand for goods and services. The explosive expansion of the domestic market spurred productivity that was continental in scope, and the economy boomed as people who came for gold stayed to become farmers, ranchers, and businessmen.

At a time when long-distance travel occurred at little more than walking pace, the sudden need for faster access and better communication and transportation systems produced astonishingly quick responses; Western Union would complete the first transcontinental telegraph line in 1861 (dooming the venerable Pony Express) and the transcontinental railroad would be completed in 1869.

And in the fastest trip to statehood in U.S. history, California became the thirty-first state in 1850. Organized government in the region had not kept pace with the explosive growth of population and industry brought on by the gold rush, and California's new settlers clamored for law and order, civil services, and the stabilization that statehood would bring, skipping the establishment of territorial government. But the successful drive for statehood caused a new problem: The Missouri Compromise of 1820 dictated a balance of free and slave states, which at the time stood at fifteen each, and California's admission to the Union as a free state upset that balance.

The Compromise of 1850 Hastens the End of the Antebellum Era

The 1850 controversy that surrounded ratification of California statehood was a crucial link in the 1840–1860 chain of events. To pacify slave-state legislators, a new compromise had been hammered out that included passage of the Fugitive Slave Act, which required citizens to help recover fugitive slaves and denied fugitives the right to a jury trial. But the act only strengthened abolitionists' resolve to put an end to slavery, and the Underground Railroad reached its peak as slaves in the North and South alike reacted to the new restrictions by attempting to flee to Canada.

By weakening shaky political compromises and deepening political division over the question of slavery in the territories, the controversy over California statehood hastened the Civil War and the end of the antebellum era. *Events That Changed the World: 1840–1860* examines the key events of this period to help readers understand not only their immediate circumstances but also their cause-and-effect connections and their cumulative, permanent consequences.

British Takeover Transforms Hong Kong

by Peter Ward Fay

During the early nineteenth century, British merchants smuggled opium from India into China. The Chinese government enacted prohibitions on opium trafficking, and in 1839, Imperial Commissioner Lin Tse-hsü (or Tse-Hs) arrived in the port of Canton to oversee the confiscation and destruction of twenty thousand chests of opium. In response, Great Britain sent gunboats to Hong Kong in 1840 and the First Opium War broke out. After two years of fighting and the capture of Shanghai, Nanking, and other cities, victorious British forces intimidated the Chinese into signing a peace treaty at Nanking in 1842.

In accordance with the terms of the treaty, China ceded Hong Kong to the British, opened five ports to British trade and residence, and were obligated to set customs duties at low levels. This "unequal treaty" was the first of several that China would be compelled to sign with Western powers. It set a precedent of special privileges for European and American traders in China. It did not, however, result in lasting peace between China and Great Britain, which fought each other again in the Second Opium War (1856–1860).

In this article, Peter Ward Fay recounts the events of the First Opium War and the wartime appeal of Hong Kong as an anchorage and opium post. He focuses on the increasing interest of the British in Hong Kong during the course of the war and the transformation

Peter Ward Fay, *The Opium War, 1840–1842: Barbarians in the Celestial Empire in the Early Part of the Nineteenth Century and the War by Which They Forced Her Gates Ajar*. Chapel Hill: University of North Carolina Press, 1997. Copyright © 1975 by the University of North Carolina Press. Reproduced by permission.

of the port since the Treaty of Nanking in 1842. Once a barren, desolate island, Hong Kong became a densely populated center of trade and commerce. It remains an important cosmopolitan city in the present day.

Peter Ward Fay was professor emeritus of history at the California Institute of Technology in Pasadena until his death in 2004. He is the author of *The Opium War, 1840–1842: Barbarians in the Celestial Empire in the Early Part of the Nineteenth Century*, from which this selection is taken.

It's a place all ups and downs, the hills rising to gaunt granite peaks, the gullies falling to narrow beaches and rocky coves. Two large islands and quite a few small ones embrace the Kowloon peninsula, which pushes gently into the South China Sea, and if you could somehow bring the land parts tidily together, you'd have a square only twenty miles on a side. So it's no more than a patch, this, possessing no natural resources; in fact, not even gifted, given the narrowness of the shoreline and the steepness of the approach, as a place nature intended for a port. A patch of ground that in the 1840s, when it first began to get attention, could point to only a handful of inhabitants, most of them farmers and fisherman, and offered no compelling reason why it should ever attract more. In short, a piece of China that on the face of it ought never to have become what today it *has* become: a place packed with over six million people, almost all of whom are Chinese, and almost none of whom farm or fish. A place well known to westerners, many of them Americans, who come and go and even settle down, brought less by the tourist attractions than by the business opportunities it offers—the money to be made—at the highest levels of commerce and finance. A place well known to a particular group among these westerners, a group brought for the same reasons but harboring a feeling—a keen and now somewhat bitter feeling—that they have always been more than visitors: they *belong* there. And a government, distant, acidly determined, that insists they never have and don't. The place, of course, is Hong Kong.

The Transformation of Hong Kong

No one looking back to the moment when Hong Kong began to make a name for itself should have expected that because it was barren and empty, barren and empty it would always be. Circumstances have a way of invalidating expectation. The circumstance in this case was a decision on the part of the British, shortly before the Opium War began, to take refuge there. Hong Kong island (eventually it passed its name on to the colony as a whole) is some eight miles long and up to four miles wide. It lies east to west just below the Kowloon peninsula and forms a "U" about Kowloon's tip but always a mile or more away. The water there is deep but the bottom is not beyond the reach of an anchor. The wind is muffled (not always—a typhoon at Hong Kong can be disastrous) on the west by Lantao, the other big island in the group, and on the east by an extension of the mainland. As a place to drop anchor in, nothing more secure is available anywhere else about the Gulf of Canton. Indeed, so effectively does the topography lock Hong Kong in that if you arrive one evening by sea, as tourists often do, when you come on deck in the morning you may wonder how your ship got in at all.

A safe anchorage—that was all the British at the time wanted. There was no thought of landing or taking on goods. The narrowness of the seafront would not have been helpful, and anyway, there were no docks or landing slips. But on a day late in August 1839, they came, several score merchant ships accompanied by the few small men-of-war available to Charles Elliot—he was the chief superintendent of trade, and in that capacity Britain's only official representative on the China coast. Besides officers and crew and men from the agency houses, the ships carried the whole of the British community—men, women, and children—at Macao. They had left at the insistence of the Portuguese governor because Chinese troops were threatening Macao from the north. In the gulf itself there had already been some bloody scraps. Off Lantao one night, boatloads of Chinese had attacked a passage schooner, killed every lascar except the bosun (who jumped into the water and clung to the rudder), and so knocked about the single English passenger—cutting off one ear and stuffing it into his mouth—that it was a mercy he survived. No doubt these had been pirates. There were many about the gulf. But war junks of the Chinese maritime service were making threatening gestures, too. And behind all this was a much more annoying development. In March, at the height of the trading season, a special high commissioner sent direct from Peking (Beijing) had reached Canton (Guangzhou), lectured the local mandarins and the Hong merchants into a state of shock, and made arrangements to bring the barbarians, particularly the British barbarians, to order. His first step had been to cut the barbarians off from all contact with Macao or their ships. His second had been to force, as a condition of their release, the surrender of merchandise worth several million dollars. Next, he had declared all further trade with the British closed until other conditions were met, conditions with which the British had made it plain they would not comply. And at the same time he had signaled, by the suddenly vigorous behavior of his war junks and troops, that if they wouldn't, they would pay.

The Start of the Opium War

The merchandise was opium, twenty thousand chests of it, brought into the gulf and up to the mouth of the Canton (or Pearl) river, surrendered there to the special high commissioner Lin Tse-Hs, and destroyed by being dumped into salt water. Twenty thousand chests worth perhaps six million dollars, or two-and-a-half million pounds sterling. Elliot had persuaded the merchants involved (Lin, no fool, had a pretty good idea who they were and how much of the stuff they had) to send for the chests. Naturally, they were not in the river, but in receiving ships (floating warehouses) out in the gulf or up the coast, or in the opium clippers that had brought them from Calcutta. Getting word to these vessels had taken time. There was a good deal of resistance to the giving of the necessary orders, in part because most of the chests belonged to distant persons who had entrusted them to these merchants to be sold. But Elliot had assured them that he asked for the surrender on behalf of his government. Surely it would find the money to cover the loss. Failing that, it would compel the Chinese to do so.

Meanwhile, the British were looking for their safe anchorage, not because they walked in fear and trembling of what Lin Tse-Hs would do now, but because they intended to make his next move impossible. He had taken them for a tidy sum by catching them up a river. He must not be allowed to catch them thus again—not him, not others, ever. Lin knew where they were. British vessels had dropped anchor at Hong Kong before and had not hesitated to meet impertinent behavior—in their confidence that was how they instinctively perceived it—with solid shot. They would not hesitate now. And if things turned violent Lin would be instantly alerted. But the Hong Kong roadstead, a mile wide, with exits at both ends and no forts save a small battery at Kowloon, was a far cry from the Canton River. He could never repeat his maneuver here.

Wisely, he did not try. As for the British, for a while they stayed on, nearly seventy vessels which, if you include their crews, meant several thousand men, some armed, all restless, living aboard ship but going ashore for water and recreation. To Jack Tar [a general epithet for sailors], going ashore no doubt meant women and drink. There were clashes. Rumor had it some of the springs were poisoned, and when three war junks suspected of directing it refused to move off, Elliot sent a cutter and two other craft and almost blew them, much larger though they were, out of the water. Was this the beginning of the war, the Opium War? In those days, formality and habit required at the start of a war a declaration to that effect, a declaration accompanied by the withdrawal of ambassadors. But neither Peking nor London had ambassadors positioned and ready to be withdrawn; Peking because it could perceive about the world no equal to whom an ambassador could possibly be sent, London because Peking could not possibly, of course, receive one. Perhaps, then, we should fix the war's opening at the moment when London decided to send an expeditionary force. Or at the moment . . . when the force arrived and made serious fighting possible.

The Wartime Appeal of Hong Kong

The force arrived in June 1840, paused briefly off the gulf, left a few ships and troops behind, and went on up the coast. Chusan was its first serious objective, direct diplomatic contact with Peking the goal. What the reader will also discover is that although the men and ships left behind recovered command of the gulf (men, women, and children went back to Macao), Hong Kong was not abandoned. On the contrary, it gradually became the anchorage of choice for men-of-war and merchant vessels both.

Its very emptiness was inviting. Men-of-war could drop anchor, load provisions, take on water, and replace canvas, rigging, and spars, free from interference or even observation on the part of the Chinese. *They*, after all, had little presence on the Kowloon side of the roadstead. They had no presence at all on the island, and made no attempt to establish any, which was not surprising given their habitual inability to take seriously barbarians who approached by sea. An attempt would have failed anyway. Reaching the roadstead by land would have proved difficult. They could not have laid out and built a proper fort, even on the Kowloon side, quickly enough to withstand what a frigate's broadsides were sure to send their way at the very first sign of the intent. But the same frigate, anchored in this roadstead, was in an excellent position to sally out instantly into the gulf, or set off up the coast. The advantages were obvious. And they corresponded nicely with what London had in mind.

For with the expeditionary force had come certain instructions from Her Majesty's Government, and among them was one that directed the establishing, somewhere along China's coast, of a base and refuge for Her Majesty's forces, perhaps temporary, but eventually to be made permanent by a formal act of cession. The why of all this was not explicit. No doubt London, however, had not forgotten what had happened a few years back to Lord Napier—peer, naval officer, and the first superintendent of trade—when he went up to Canton and (among other things) tried to approach the governor-general directly. The governor-general had not taken kindly to this. He had ordered Napier away, and when he would not leave, forcibly confined him to the factories. Napier had two frigates at the Bogue. He summoned them up. With some difficulty they got as far as Whampoa, within sight of the factories, but there their own deep draft, and the sight of chop boats weighted with rocks (being sunk in a way calculated to trap them), gave their skippers pause. They went no farther. Napier hung on a little longer and then, sick and dispirited, let himself be sent down slowly, almost alone, and by a devious route. Within hours of reaching Macao he was dead.

Possession of Hong Kong

Napier was surely not forgotten. In London the humiliation had inflamed, among others, the Duke of Wellington. But this was not the first time an effort to meet the Middle Kingdom on equal terms had failed, and the cost—one man's death—cannot have seemed exorbitant. Not so the cost, even if measured simply in pounds, shillings, and pence, of the forcible confinement a little more than a year back of the entire British merchant community at the very same place. The expeditionary force had been sent to China to efface that unjust and humiliating act, and to recover the value of the confiscated chests plus expenses. It could not, of course, remain on the China coast forever. A secure enclave was necessary while the task of coaxing or forcing China into relations of equal-

ity and openness went forward. And Hong Kong, it seemed to Elliot and others on the spot, would do nicely.

Without waiting, therefore, for Her Majesty's Government to
specify the when and where of the required enclave, Sir Gordon
Bremer, the senior naval officer on the station, took formal possession of Hong Kong in Britain's name on January 26, 1841, at a
little promontory thereafter known as Possession Point. Her
Majesty's Government was not altogether pleased when it heard.
The island as described struck Lord Palmerston, the foreign secretary, as rather a barren place, which of course it was. A small group
of Protestant missionaries, who came over from Macao to look
around, thought as little of its prospects. "A continued chain of un-
couth, naked, rocky, poor, uncultivated, and uncultivable mountains," one is reported to have said. But there was no going back on
Bremer's action. The naval officers were happy with the selection.

So were the merchants. If the anchorage was useful for men-
of-war, it was even more useful for their opium ships. The traffic
in that commodity had never required warehousing on a large
scale. A careful selection among samples, a leisurely bargaining
over price, and the other ordinary procedures of trade in teas, cotton, and the like had not been required. Opium's bulk was modest, relatively speaking. If packed properly it did not spoil. Best of
all, as long as the demand was high, you did not have to go looking for customers: they came to you, paid you on the spot in silver, and went away with what they had ordered. Your only worry
was interference by pirate or mandarin boats, and for that you
armed your vessels well. But if you lay in an anchorage that men-
of-war frequented, so much the better—they would lend you a
fighting hand. Hong Kong was such. With its possession now formal, the merchants should be able to expand. "Elliot says that he
sees no objection to our storing opium there," James Matheson
wrote to one of the Jardines, "and as soon as the New Year holi-
days are over I shall set about building." Build he did. Others, who
like Matheson did business in much more than just the drug, built
too. Before the Opium War was over, the north shore of the island
boasted a road some four miles in length, with a straggling ribbon
of a town along it. The mat sheds of the Chinese were relieved
from time to time by houses built of a mixture of clay, lime, and
broken stone, the whole pounded between wooden forms. There
were even a few bungalows and godowns in granite or brick.

Hong Kong and opium. The place, the British, the drug. A natural, deadly, three-way symbiosis. The one inconceivable without the other two, particularly if you have been listening to what official China tells us and whole masses of Chinese believe. Hong Kong itself had a dose of this as the appointed surrender, scheduled to take place on the last day of June 1997, came near. The theme was homecoming. Taking Hong Kong back from the British was to be a homecoming, not just for the Hong Kong Chinese but for Chinese everywhere. Homecoming "driven home without pause" (reported Ian Buruma of the *New York Review Of Books*, who was there), "in official speeches, a new movie, mass stadium demonstrations, newspaper headlines, buttons and badges, T-shirts and posters, and slogans in wooden Chinese." The homecoming was to be a patriotic victory that wiped out 150 years of humiliation and shame inflicted by the British and the despicable native hucksters through whom they did their smuggling. For it was at Hong Kong, seized impudently and brazenly so many, many years ago, that the British had pushed for so long, and with such dreadful consequences to China's millions, their unconscionable traffic in opium.

Nanking Is in Danger

by Imperial Commissioner Ch-i-Ying, Deputy Lieutenant General Yilipu, and Governor-General Niu Ken

Great Britain and China signed the Treaty of Nanking, ending the First Opium War on August 29, 1842. This document is a report to the Chinese emperor from the Chinese government officials holding posts in the region where the fighting took place. The memorial, as the on site report is called, captures the mood of the officials and the pressures they encountered in the days leading up to the peace agreement. In early August the British made various demands, including monetary compensation, cession of Hong Kong, and national equality in official communication with China's government. The officials who drafted this document emphasize that according to the British, acquiescing to these demands will end hostilities whereas refusing them will escalate fighting. The British troops took Nanking in a show of force. The Chinese authors take the British threats seriously. Because they are mediators whose role is to advise the emperor, the officials not only posit but recommend negotiation as an alternative to continued hostility. The demands, as the government representatives see them, are greedy but otherwise without ill intent.

On the eighth day of this month [August 13, 1842], we, your ministers, made a joint memorial reporting the story of the management of barbarians' [England's] affairs. The

---

Imperial Commissioner Ch-i-Ying, Deputy Lieutenant General Yilipu, and Governor-General Niu Ken, "The English Threaten the Chinese Officials at Nanking with Force," *A Critical Study of the First Anglo-Chinese War: With Documents*, edited by P.C. Kuo. Shanghai, China: The Commercial Press, 1935.

day preceding that [August 12, 1842], the said barbarians made a list of their demands, and the list was brought back to us by our commissioner Tafengpu.

British Demands

We found that the first of their demands was to have 21,000,000 dollars in foreign currency from us. Of that sum 6,000,000 should be paid in the present year, and the rest in annual installments. The second was the demand to have Hongkong to be their port. And, in addition, they asked to have the privilege to trade at Canton, Fuchow, Amoy, Ningpo, and Shanghai. The third demand was the principle of national equality in official communications with the Chinese government. Although there were other demands, yet these three were the fundamental points.

They emphatically declared that if these demands were complied with, they will have peace and amity with us and will never start any hostilities. But, if these demands should be refused, they will fight, and also will go to invade other provinces.

Just when we were conferring on the measures to be taken in reply to this, the barbarians suddenly flew a red flag and mounted huge cannons on Chung-shan. It was about eight o'clock P.M. on the eighth day of the month [August 13, 1842], and the occasion for the action was the rumor that we had called hither the troops of Shechung to attack them. The barbarians declared that they were ready to assault the city on the morrow, and their temper was very rough.

Nanking in Danger

We found that although there were troops garrisoning the city of Nanking, yet the circumference of the metropolis amounts to more than fifty li [a Chinese unit of distance equal to about one-third mile], and the troops we had were not sufficiently strong. Furthermore, the forces that came from Kiangsi, Hupeh, and Hsüchow had met defeat before, and consequently they had little *esprit de corps.* We dared not to rely upon them. Besides, Chung-shan is so near to the metropolis that, should the barbarians once fire from the heights, it is certain that we cannot stand it even for a brief moment. The sentiment among the people here was feeble. When they caught wind of the threatened attack, they seethed with panic and fear. Instantly, tens of thousands of men and women crowded to our yamen [government headquarters], filling the streets and crying for rescue.

Since the barbarians began to flout our authority, they have gone from Canton to Fukien, thence to Chekiang, and finally up the Yangtze river. The troops sent by us had all failed to check their advance. Now they assembled a great number of rotten people, and their ships numbered more than eighty. With these men and vessels they captured Chinkiang, dominated the Yangtze river, and cut off our communication between the north and the south. And, at present, they have all advanced to besiege Nanking, which is consequently in imminent danger. We have seen the critical conditions direct. Should we still persist in resistance and should the city fall to the barbarians, the loss of our own lives is an insignificant matter. But we fear that once this city, the metropolis of three provinces, should be upset, not only would the route to Chinkiang be cut off, but the barbarians could easily sail direct to the capitals of Anhwei, Kiangsi, and Hupeh. Moreover, according to a report of the magistrate of Yangchow, Pang I-chu, the barbarians had declared that if they fight and lose, they will employ native traitors to instigate troubles from within. Should this be true, the disaster would be still more inconceivable.

No Dark Schemes

We believe that, although the demands of the barbarians are indeed rapacious, yet they are little more than a desire for ports and for the privilege of trade. There are no dark schemes in them. Compared with war which will inevitably entail great disasters, we would rather see assent be given to their demands, and thus save the whole country south of the Yangtze.

We have sent a communication to the barbarians binding upon them the agreement that if they repent and stop fighting, we will presently negotiate with them according to the conditions they proposed, and that meantime we will petition the favor of your Majesty to give assent thereto. But should the animal temper of the barbarians still refuse to obey these commands, we have only one alternative, and that is to stir up our soldiers and officers to make a last defense of the city. We would not consider what might be the consequences, victory or defeat.

The Communication Revolution Began with Morse's Invention

by Daniel A. Wren and Ronald G. Greenwood

In 1837 Samuel F.B. Morse patented his invention, the telegraph. This machine worked by sending clicking signals over a wire, based on an alphabetical code devised by Morse. Congress was impressed by Morse's invention and funded an effort to place a test cable between Baltimore, Maryland, and Washington, D.C. On May 24, 1844, the first telegraph message was sent over a distance. The biblical phrase, "What hath God wrought!" was the message transmitted over forty miles from the Supreme Court in Washington to Baltimore.

In the following selection, Daniel A. Wren and Ronald G. Greenwood write that the "communication revolution" began with Morse's telegraph. The authors note that success of the telegraph ultimately inspired other communication pioneers such as telephone inventor Alexander Graham Bell to work on new technology. According to Wren and Greenwood, the telegraph had a greater impact on American business in the nineteenth century than any other development aside from railroads. The first successful telegraph transmission was quickly followed by the establishment of telegraph companies and construction of lines across the country. Distance was now measured by time intervals as well as miles. Wren and Greenwood explain that because telegraph cables were often placed along railroad rights-of-way, a close relationship evolved between transportation and communication. The authors note that when Morse died in 1872, his invention was recognized as the world's standard for telecommunication.

Daniel A. Wren is a retired professor of management at the University of Oklahoma in Oklahoma, where he is currently curator of the Harry W. Bass Business History Collection. Ronald G. Greenwood taught management history at the University of Wisconsin in Madison and several other institutions. Both authors have written a number of books on the history of management.

I n 490 BC, Pheidippides carried the news of the Greek victory over the invading Persian army at Marathon to Athens, a distance of some twenty-two miles, in three hours. It is told that this messenger gasped the news to his audience but then fell dead of his exertion. The story of this early messenger illustrates the primitive reliance on humans, animals, or other natural forces for communicating over long distances. Messengers and commerce appear hand in hand historically, representing the reliance of business on means of communication. Indeed, Mercury, the Latin god of commerce, portrayed as wearing a winged hat, was also the messenger of the gods and the god of eloquence.

The Communication Revolution

Other than a national network of railroads, no development had as much impact on U.S. business in the nineteenth century as the telegraph. The telegraph enabled a rapid exchange of messages over long distances, quickly and cheaply, connecting buyers, sellers, and transporters. Without the telegraph, a national and international market would not have emerged as quickly as it did. The communication revolution began with Samuel F.B. Morse and his telegraph, a quantum leap in information technology. Ezra Cornell built and promoted the telegraph, and he saw the need for consolidation, but fell prey to the intrigues of an emerging industry. Finally, Alexander Graham Bell represents another advancement in communicating over distances, the telephone, which came to rival the telegraph. Bell was an inventor, but, more important, he was also an entrepreneur.

The forces of electricity and magnetism were known since ancient times but it was not until the early 1800s that Hans Christian Oersted discovered that electricity could travel by wire and produce a magnetic effect at a terminal. By switching the current on and off a magnetic charge or discharge could be effected. Other scientists such as Michael Faraday, James Maxwell, Alessandro Volta, and Sir William Thomson (Lord Kelvin) became interested in this phenomenon, but it appears that André-Marie Ampère was the first to suggest that electro-magnetism could be used for "distance signaling."

Scientists in Britain and Europe were working on transmitting electromagnetic impulses by wire in the 1830s. While in Europe a young portrait painter and inventor, Samuel F.B. Morse, became intrigued with these ideas, especially Ampère's distance signaling. Morse was born in Charleston, Massachusetts, on April 27, 1791, the son of Jedediah and Elizabeth Ann Breese Morse. Samuel studied "natural philosophy," which included classes in electricity and chemistry, at Yale College, but his ambition was to be an artist. It was his trip abroad in 1832 to seek portrait commissions that brought him into contact with the scientific work there.

Returning from Europe, Morse devised a code of dots and dashes that represented letters of the alphabet. These marks would appear on a moving strip of paper at a terminal in response to electromagnetic impulses sent by wire. Morse developed the idea in 1832 but did not patent it until 1837 as the electromagnetic recording telegraph. In that same year William Cooke and Charles Wheatstone obtained a British patent and installed thirteen miles of wires on poles along the Great Western Railroad, a German named Steinheil demonstrated distance signaling from Munich to a nearby village, and others were gaining patents. A great legal battle was about to begin.

The First Telegraph Transmission

Initial capital came from Alfred Vail, the son of a successful iron works owner in Morristown, New Jersey. Vail had seen Morse demonstrate his telegraph, saw its potential, and borrowed money from his father for a one-fourth interest in developing it. In 1838 Morse strung three miles of wires and transmitted the message "A patient waiter is no loser" throughout the interior of the Speedwell Iron Works.

Morse and Vail wished to demonstrate further the telegraph and sought financial support from Congress. The plan was to insert insulated copper wires in lead pipes that would be laid in a trench to be dug between the dual track lines of the Baltimore and Ohio Railroad between Baltimore and Washington, D.C. Morse was appropriated his estimated cost of $25,420 and he began his original plan with a young mechanic, Ezra Cornell, inventing a ditch-digging machine that would also cover the pipe after it was installed. Early in the project, it was discovered that the lead pipes leaked badly, allowing water to soak through the insulation and disrupt the electrical flow.

After considerable discussion it was decided to follow the British example and place the wires on poles. More money was needed for poles, hole digging, pole insulators, and so on, so Morse went back to Congress, finally getting his total appropriation increased to $30,000. Morse may have been the first federal contractor to incur a cost overrun.

Construction was finally completed, and the first telegraphic

Samuel F.B. Morse (center) reenacts transmitting the very first telegraphic message in 1844.

message over a longer distance was transmitted from the chamber of the U.S. Supreme Court in Washington, D.C., to Baltimore, Maryland, a distance of some forty miles, on May 24, 1844. The message was from the Old Testament: "What hath God wrought" (Numbers 23:23).

Once demonstrated, the problem was what to do to further develop the telegraph. Congress appropriated $8,000 to operate the telegraph and placed responsibility for it in the postmaster general's office. Morse offered his patent rights to the government for $100,000. This notion was rejected by the postmaster general, Cave Johnson, who had earlier pronounced the telegraph as "unworthy of the notice of sensible men." In its first year of operation the Washington-Baltimore line lost money, reinforcing Johnson's opinion that the telegraph's revenues could never "be made equal to its expenditures" under any circumstances. Johnson's myopia brought history's good fortune—the telegraph would be a private enterprise and not part of the U.S. Postal Service.

The Effects of Morse's Invention

Morse formed the Magnetic Telegraph Company, appointed a former postmaster general, Amos Kendall, as his attorney and business manager, and spent the next ten years defending his patent, refining his invention, and traveling and promoting the telegraph. There were numerous rivals in the United States and abroad, but the Morse patents of 1837, 1840, and 1846 stood legal test after test until the U.S. Supreme Court upheld Morse's rights in 1854.

The Magnetic Telegraph Company had started the business, but Amos Kendall was licensing the Morse patent to numerous others, who began to build lines across the United States to the Mississippi River. In 1855 there were an estimated twenty-five electric telegraph companies in various locales. Messages were not cheap: 50¢ for ten words, and 5¢ for each additional word, rates that were affordable primarily by commercial ventures. The report of an 1855 committee indicated the changes that were occurring:

> The advantages to be derived from the adoption of the Electric Telegraph, have in no country been more promptly appreciated than in the United States. A system of communication that annihilates distance was felt to be of vital importance, both politically and commercially, in a country so vast, and having a population so widely scattered. . . .

> Distances are now to be measured by intervals, not of space, but of time: to bring Boston, New York, and Philadelphia into instantaneous communication with New Orleans and St. Louis—In the operations of commerce, the great capitals of the North, South, and West are moved, as it were, by a common intelligence; information respecting the state of the various markets is readily obtained, the results of consignments may be calculated almost with certainty, and sudden fluctuations in price in a great measure provided against.

Typically built along railroad rights-of-way, the telegraph and the railroads formed the earliest connections to integrate transportation and communication. On the New York and Erie, for example, the telegraph line was built in 1848 and used for dispatching trains. When Daniel McCallum became superintendent of that line in 1854, he developed information management to what was probably the highest state of the art for the times. He used the telegraph to make operations safer as well as to facilitate administration by requiring hourly reports to show the position of every train in the system, daily reports on passengers and cargo, and monthly reports to give management statistical accounts for planning, rate making, and control.

In 1854 a submarine cable crossed the Gulf of St. Lawrence to connect Nova Scotia and Newfoundland. Morse bragged that now Europe was "within six days of America," that is, the telegraph to Newfoundland and six days on a steamer to Galway, Ireland. October 1861 saw the completion of the first transcontinental line, joined in Salt Lake City—the express ponies could now retire. After five failures, Cyrus W. Field completed the Atlantic transoceanic cable in 1866, bringing San Francisco just a lightning flash away from Europe. Despite the speed of telegraphy, messages still had to be encoded, transmitted, and decoded by humans at the receiving point, where Mercury's messengers still delivered them to the addressee.

Samuel F.B. Morse died on April 2, 1872, his patents upheld and his invention honored throughout the United States, Britain, and Europe as the world's standard for telecommunications. No one could have imagined that from the message "What hath God wrought," a century and a quarter later the signal would be "That's one small step for a man, one giant leap for mankind."

2 The First Telegraph Message Is Sent:
May 24, 1844

Morse Reflects on the Success of His Telegraph

by Samuel F.B. Morse

Samuel F.B. Morse (1791–1872), once a highly regarded portrait painter, achieved fame though his invention of the telegraph. In 1832 a chance conversation about experiments with electromagnetism started Morse thinking about the notion of electrically sending messages through wires. Morse spent the next few years developing prototype instruments for the practical application of his idea. He also created a signal code for communicating with the device. By 1837 Morse had devised and patented the telegraph. That same year he applied for a grant from Congress to construct a telegraph system. After several more years of experimentation, Morse successfully sent the first message, "What hath God wrought!" on May 24, 1844, from Baltimore to Washington, D.C.

In the following letters, Morse reveals his sentiments about his telegraph project both before and after its public and commercial success. Morse attributes his good luck to God, and reflects on the significance of the sentence "What hath God wrought!"

*M*arch 23. [In a letter to his brother, Sidney, Morse states] My Telegraph labors go on well at present. The whole matter is now critical, or, as our good father used to say, 'a crisis is at hand.' I hope for the best while I endeavor to prepare my mind for the worst. . . .

Samuel F.B. Morse, *Samuel F.B. Morse: His Letters and Journals, Volume II*, edited and supplemented by Edward Lind Morse. Boston: Houghton Mifflin, 1914.

Progress of the Telegraph

April 10. A brighter day is dawning upon me. I send you the Intelligencer of to-day, in which you will see that the Telegraph is successfully under way. Through six miles the experiment has been most gratifying. In a few days I hope to advise you of more respecting it. I have preferred reserve until I could state something positive. I have my posts set to Beltsville, twelve miles, and you will see by the Intelligencer that I am prepared to go directly on to Baltimore and hope to reach there by the middle of May.

May 7 . . . You will see by the papers that the Telegraph is in successful operation for twenty-two miles, to the Junction of the Annapolis road with the Baltimore and Washington road. The nomination of Mr. Frelinghuysen as Vice-President was written, sent on, and the receipt acknowledged back in two minutes and one second, a distance of forty-four miles. The news was spread all over Washington one hour and four minutes before the cars containing the news by express arrived. In about a fortnight I hope to be in Baltimore, and a communication will be established between the two cities. Good-bye. I am almost asleep from exhaustion, so excuse abrupt closing. . . .

Success of the Telegraph

It was with well-earned but modest satisfaction that he wrote to his brother Sidney on May 31:—

You will see by the papers how great success has attended the first efforts of the Telegraph. That sentence of Annie Ellsworth's was divinely indited, for it is in my thoughts day and night. 'What hath God wrought!' It is his work, and He alone could have carried me thus far through all my trials and enabled me to triumph over the obstacles, physical and moral, which opposed me.

'Not unto us, not unto us, but to thy name, O Lord, be all the praise.'

I begin to fear now the effects of public favor, lest it should kindle that pride of heart and self-sufficiency which dwells in my own as well as in others' breasts, and which, alas! is so ready to be inflamed by the slightest spark of praise. I do indeed feel gratified, and it is right I should rejoice, but I rejoice with fear, and I desire that a sense of dependence upon and increased obligation to the Giver of every good and perfect gift may keep me humble and circumspect.

The conventions at Baltimore happened most opportunely for

the display of the powers of the Telegraph, especially as it was the means of correspondence, in one instance, between the Democratic Convention and the first candidate elect for the Vice-Presidency. The enthusiasm of the crowd before the window of the Telegraph Room in the Capitol was excited to the highest pitch at the announcement of the nomination of the Presidential candidate, and the whole of it afterwards seemed turned upon the Telegraph. They gave the Telegraph three cheers, and I was called to make my appearance at the window when three cheers were given to me by some hundreds present, composed mainly of members of Congress.

Such is the feeling in Congress that many tell me they are ready to grant anything. Even the most inveterate opposers have changed to admirers, and one of them, Hon. Cave Johnson, who ridiculed my system last session by associating it with the tricks of animal magnetism, came to me and said: 'Sir, I give in. It is an astonishing invention.'

When I see all this and such enthusiasm everywhere manifested, and contrast the present with the past season of darkness and almost despair, have I not occasion to exclaim 'What hath God wrought'? Surely none but He who has all hearts in His hands, and turns them as the rivers of waters are turned could so have brought light out of darkness. 'Sorrow may continue for a night, but joy cometh in the morning.' Pray for me then, my dear brother, that I may have a heart to praise the great Deliverer, and in future, when discouraged or despairing, be enabled to remember His past mercy, and in full faith rest all my cares on Him who careth for us.

The Famine Damaged English-Irish Relations

by John O'Beirne Ranelagh

The most dramatic episode of mass starvation in the nineteenth century was the Irish potato famine. Although the recorded dates of the famine vary, the initial trigger for the famine took place in 1845, with the years 1846–1850 marked by the worst suffering.

In 1845 more than 2 million acres of potatoes, a staple crop, were planted in Ireland. However, a fungus from North America and a change in climate yielded a potato blight rather than a harvest. Failed harvests throughout Europe caused food prices to soar. Many Irish farmers with a diseased potato crop were then unable to pay rent to their landlords, especially after the crop failed again in 1846.

Poverty, starvation, and sickness profoundly affected Ireland in the late 1840s and early 1850s. The British government did provide relief, but many Irish considered assistance too little and too late. The famine was ultimately a major factor in the depopulation of Ireland, Irish emigration, and deteriorating Irish-English relations for the remainder of the nineteenth century, fueling the Irish independence movement.

The following excerpt by John O'Beirne Ranelagh describes both the suffering brought on by the famine in Ireland and the lasting consequences of the potato blight. Ranelagh employs statistics to illustrate the population decline that resulted from deaths—over 1 million people in ten years—and emigration. Irish bitterness toward

John O'Beirne Ranelagh, *A Short History of Ireland*. Cambridge, England: Cambridge University Press, 1983. Copyright © 1983 by Telstore. Reproduced by permission of Cambridge University Press.

England, the author says, is one of the most enduring effects of the famine in Ireland.

John O'Beirne Ranelagh is the author of *A Short History of Ireland.*

The 1841 census divided the 8,175,124 people of Ireland into four categories according to their relative wealth: property owners and farmers of more than fifty acres; artisans and farmers with between five and fifty acres; labourers and small-holders with up to five acres, and the numerically insignificant fourth category, 'means unspecified'. Seventy per cent of the rural population were in the category of labourers and smallholders with five acres or less. They were spread throughout the country in three distinct patterns: a prosperous farming class and poor labouring class in the midlands and the south; a prosperous east and north, and an extremely poor and numerous class of impoverished smallholders in the west and south-western seaboard counties. The effects of the great famine reflected this pattern, with the west and south-west of the country hardest hit, and the labouring and impoverished smallholding groups bearing the brunt of starvation, sickness and death. Fever followed famine, and people all over the country died from its effects, but as far as death from starvation was concerned, the labouring population suffered almost to the exclusion of other groups. Thus in the midlands and the south, the prosperous farming class of people did not starve during the years of the 'Great Hunger'. The famine was never general in the rural community.

Failure of the Potato Crop

Between 1841 and 1851 the population fell by nearly 20 per cent to 6,552, 385. Total deaths were estimated by the census commissioners in the same period at 1,383,350—certainly an under-estimate since where whole families died, no returns were made, and not until 1864 was registration of births, marriages and deaths made compulsory. The census commissioners estimated that another 1,445,587 Irish people emigrated, mostly to America, in the same period.

The direct cause of the famine and its attendant demographic repercussions was the persistent failure of the potato crop in the years 1845 and 1846, and in the partial failure of the crop in each of the succeeding five years. By tradition, Sir Walter Raleigh is credited with the introduction of the potato to Ireland from America in 1586. Within two centuries it had become the principal vegetable food of the peasantry. It needed little labour to plant and harvest. It yielded a large amount on a small acreage, and so was ideally suited to the small tenant farmer. Together with buttermilk, it provided sufficient nutrition to sustain life and a reasonable state of health. By 1845 it had become the sole food of about one-third of the people, and bread, meat, grain or corn meal graced only the tables of the better off. Thus the effect of a potato crop failure could be devastating, and the effect of consecutive failures could be fatally destructive famine on a very large scale.

Famine had already struck in Ireland many times during the nineteenth century: in 1807, 1817, 1821–2, 1830–4, 1836, and 1839. However, while always accompanied by death and emigration, potato crop failure and famine had also always been localized. In 1845 the first signs of potato crop failure came in September when discolouration on the leaves of potato plants was noticed. When the crop was dug in October, hopes that failure would be small-scale and localized as in previous years were dashed, as over most of the country reports came in that there was no crop at all. The actual cause of the failure was *phytophthora infestans*—potato blight. The spores of the blight were carried by wind, rain and insects and came to Ireland from Britain and the European continent. A fungus growth affected the potato plants, producing black spots and a white mould on the leaves, soon rotting the potato into a pulp. The following year, the blight was general, and by the beginning of 1847 it was clear that a disaster of unprecedented magnitude was under way. Despite the fact that there was no blight in 1847, because of the small supply of seed potatoes the healthy crop that year merely reduced the extent of famine, it did not end mass starvation. Typhus, dysentery, scurvy, hunger oedema and relapsing fever ('Yellow Fever') brought death to areas of the country which had escaped the worst in the previous years. In 1848 there was widespread, though partial, crop failure again. In December, an outbreak of Asiatic cholera began which lasted until July 1849. Hundreds of thousands of people in various stages of starvation died from this and other fevers during the height of the famine, nearly all of them from the poorest section of the community, the small tenants and landless labourers. By the summer of 1847, three million people, nearly half the population of Ireland, were being fed by private charities—often organized by the Quakers—or at public expense. So many people died in so short a period of time, that mass graves were provided, often in ground specially consecrated for the purpose. Emigration soared from 75,000 in 1845 to 250,000 in 1851. Thousands of emigrants died during the Atlantic crossing (in 1847 there were 17,465 documented deaths) in 'coffin ships' plying a speculative trade, often little more than rotting bulks. Thousands more died of sickness at disembarkation centres.

The famine lasted in one part of the country or another from 1845 to 1849, with its effects lasting much longer still. The 1851 census revealed greatly enlarged urban population, numerous workhouse inmates, and large numbers of people in receipt of outdoor relief, especially in the west and the poorer parts of the country. In the west, the famine had struck hardest. There, since the time of Cromwell the bulk of the population had been concentrated. In Co. Mayo in 1841, for example, there were 475 people for every acre of arable land, and in the province of Connaught as a whole, 64 per cent of the farms were smaller than five acres. Through these congested districts, famine diseases spread like wildfire.

The British Government's Response

The danger of famine inherent in dependence upon one particular source of food had not escaped the awareness of the government in London. A century earlier, in 1740–1, a previous famine had resulted in the deaths of an estimated 400,000 Irishmen. In 1832 famine had been accompanied by cholera. At the same time, the political philosophy of the day was *laissez-faire*, the belief in the efficacy of the unrestrained forces of the market in all circumstances, and in common with nineteenth-century European political practice, British political parties were all wedded to it. Nevertheless, the response of the Tory government under Sir Robert Peel in 1845–6 was prompt, efficient and interventionist.

Sir Robert Peel (1788–1850) was a politician noted for his dedication to administrative efficiency. Born in Lancashire, the son of a textile mill-owner, Peel entered politics in 1809 as an Irish Tory MP for Cashel, Co. Tipperary. In 1812 he was appointed chief secretary for Ireland, serving for six years—the longest of any chief secretary of the century. His tenure of office in Ireland was marked by the animosity Peel and Daniel O'Connell had for each other (O'Connell dubbed him 'Orange Peel', referred to him as 'a raw youth, squeezed out of I know not what factory in England', and was challenged to a duel by Peel in 1815), and by the imaginative—almost experimental—nature of his policies. He created in 1814 a police force, the Peace Preservation Police, quickly known as 'Peelers'; the following year he created a precedent by establishing a state grant for primary education, and during the famine of 1817 he demonstrated his flexibility and willingness to flout the common wisdom of the day by providing £250,000 for relief works. In 1829 he led in the debate on Catholic emancipation, supporting it in the house of commons while the prime minister, the duke of Wellington, supported it in the lords. Prime minister himself from 1834 to 35 and again from 1841 to 46, Peel showed himself willing to concede reform, but unwilling to consider constitutional changes, and he steadfastly opposed O'Connell's Repeal Association. In 1845 he granted an annual endowment of £26,000 to the Catholic seminary, Maynooth College, and introduced the non-denominational Queen's Colleges—the first state-created university colleges in British history—in an attempt to open higher education to Catholics. By the end of the year, growing famine distress in Ireland had convinced him of the need immediately to abolish the Corn Laws (tariffs on grain imported into the United Kingdom which in effect subsidized UK farmers) so as to lower the price of corn and therefore bread. The strong farming and landowning interests in the Tory Party opposed their leader on this issue. Peel persevered, splitting his Party and losing office the following year when, with Opposition Whig support, he forced the repeal of the Corn Laws through parliament: Benjamin Disraeli, the young Tory MP for Maidenhead, leapt to prominence and ultimately the leadership of the Conservative Party by spearheading the revolt against Peel on this issue.

Repeal of the Corn Laws was only one of several measures Peel applied to relieve the effects of famine. In November 1845 he appointed a scientific commission to decide what should be done: they incorrectly diagnosed the nature of the potato blight, and so were ineffective, but this was not Peel's fault. He himself recognized that the first priority had to be the provision of food, and he personally authorized (without cabinet approval) the purchase of £100,000 of maize from the United States for distribution in Ireland by a Relief Commission he set up to coordinate relief work. To provide employment and thus money for starving Irishmen to buy food, early in 1846 he secured the passage of Acts which authorized improvements for Irish harbours and roads. He encouraged voluntary relief committees (about 650 were formed by August 1846) and established special food depots which released food supplies on to the open market so as to ensure that local traders would not be able to raise prices and capitalize on misery. Altogether, his policies worked: no one died from starvation alone while Peel was in office.

Alleviation Measures

Having split his Party over the repeal of the Corn Laws, Peel was voted out of office at the end of June 1846. His successor as prime minister, the Whig Lord John Russell, came into office just as it was becoming clear that, for the first time, the whole potato crop of Ireland was blighted. Part of Peel's success in dealing with the famine lay in the fact that the 1845 crop failure was only partial. In 1846, Ireland was faced with famine of an altogether greater magnitude. This was compounded by Russell. Unlike Peel, who had pragmatically concentrated upon ensuring that there was enough food to feed those in desperate need, Russell was a doctrinaire exponent of *laissez-faire*. He also headed a minority government, dependent upon the votes of Tories who had found Peel too liberal. So, while the Whigs had supported Peel over the repeal of the Corn Laws, and while Russell himself had a liberal record, in order to stay in office he found it necessary to stick to political principles generally acceptable to Tories. In October 1846 he set out his approach to the famine: 'It must be thoroughly understood that we cannot feed the people. . . . We can at best keep down prices where there is no regular market and prevent established dealers from raising prices much beyond the fair price with ordinary profits.' His policies emphasized employment rather than food for famine victims in the belief that private enterprise, not government, should be responsible for food provision, and that the cost of Irish relief work should be paid for by Irishmen. Peel's Relief Commission was abolished, and all public relief work was put in the hands of the 12,000 civil servants in the Board of Works who manfully tried to find work for nearly 750,000 starving people on top of all their normal responsibilities. Workhouses were built where, in return for hard (and often pointless) work, starving peasants were paid starvation wages. Tens of thousands of people died during the winter of 1846, forcing the government to accept that its policies were not working and that Peel's policy of state intervention in food supply and distribution was the only alternative. In March 1847, Russell authorized the general distribution of food to the destitute. No one who held as much as a quarter of an acre could qualify, however, with the result that hundreds of thousands gave up their holdings in order not to starve.

Private enterprise also contributed significantly to the alleviation of distress. Many individual landlords did the best they could for their tenants. Soup kitchens, freely feeding starving peasants, were established by landlords and notably by the Society of Friends and the British Relief Association. Unfortunately, some evangelical Anglican clergymen, particularly in the west of Ireland, brought distrust to the notion of soup kitchens with 'Souperism': offering nourishment to people in return for their conversion. Early in 1847, government-sponsored soup kitchens were established, and by August that year 3,000,000 people a day were being fed by them. But Russell and his colleagues never conceived of interfering with the structure of the Irish economy in the ways that would have been necessary to prevent the worst effects of the famine. There was no attempt to reform tenancies or agricultural practices. Instead, landlords (who were responsible for the rates of their tenants on holdings valued at £4 or less, even if rents were not paid) in some cases evicted tenants as a way of reducing rate bills (in 1850, 104,000 people were evicted), and farmers and merchants were able to export grain and cattle without government hindrance. One of the most remarkable facts about the famine period is that an average £100,000 of food was exported from Ireland every month: almost throughout, Ireland remained a net exporter of food.

In addition to private and government intervention, the Poor Law unions administered the bulk of relief work. The 130 unions in Ireland had been introduced in 1838 with the Irish Poor Law Act, extending the British Poor Law system to Ireland. Under his system each union was supervised by a Board of Guardians consisting of local ratepayers, responsible for workhouses where the destitute could work in exchange for subsistence wages. The unions were supported by local rates, and as a result whole districts were bankrupted through the unions' expenditure during the famine. In an attempt both to contain such bankruptcy and to extend workhouse relief, in 1847 the government increased the number of unions to 162. The extent of their work can be judged by the numbers employed in relief works: 114,600 in October 1846; 570,000 in January 1847 and 734,000 in March. Over £7 million was spent by the government in grants and loans during the famine, much of this through the Poor Law unions. . . .

Varied Consequences of the Famine

The long-term consequences of the famine were varied and tremendous. The most notable was the tradition it firmly established of emigration, principally to the United States of America. Between 1845 and 1855, nearly two million people had emigrated from Ireland to America and Australia, and another 750,000 to Britain. By 1900 over four million Irishmen had crossed the Atlantic, and as many lived abroad as in Ireland. In the century up to 1930, it is estimated that one out of every two people born in Ireland emigrated. Between 1951 and 1961, net emigration from the country as a whole amounted to 437,682. Since then, emigration has fallen substantially, but it is still an element in Irish life.

There were other drastic consequences too. Potatoes declined rapidly in importance as the remaining farmers and tenants in Ireland after the famine changed over from tillage to grazing sheep and cattle. This in turn ended the practice of farm subdivision, and one son came generally to inherit farms intact. Emigration or a threadbare existence were the choices facing younger children, and practically every census between 1851 and 1961 showed a decline in Ireland's population (a 0.46 per cent population increase was reported in 1936–7, and an increase of 1.96 per cent shown in 1951). Part of the population loss reflected the increasing age at which Irish people in the main began to marry: in 1900 in rural Ireland the average age at marriage for men was thirty-nine and for women thirty-one. Late marriage was a characteristic of the Irish farming community before the famine, with only the labouring/cottier class enjoying early marriage. After the famine, the labouring/cottier class (which was hit hardest) was much reduced, and farmers became the largest single class on the land, a phenomenon reflected not only in the characteristic of late marriage, but also in a change in the nature of land-ownership. Indeed, the famine affected the farming community only slightly, and it emerged strengthened as a consequence. As labourers and cottiers died or emigrated, leaving their small-holdings, so small farmers extended their plots. In 1845 there had been nearly 630,000 holdings of up to fifteen acres (with each holding basically supporting a family); by 1851 there were only 318,000. In the same period, the number of holdings of fifteen acres or more increased from 277,000 to 290,000.

The famine also ended the widespread use of the Irish language. Gaelic, the natural language of 4 million Irish people in 1841, by 1851 was spoken only by 1.7 million; in 1911 by only 527,000. 'The Famine', wrote Douglas Hyde in 1891, 'knocked the heart out of the Irish language.' Speaking Irish had become firmly identified with poverty and peasanthood, with famine and death. In the later decades of the nineteenth century, Irish-speaking parents joined wholeheartedly with priests and teachers to force their children to speak only English. English was identified with success and well-being. It was the language of commerce, and the language of emigrant relatives too. The 1831 National Education Act established English as the language of Ireland's first national primary-school system. Hedge-school teachers before the National Schools were introduced had used tally-sticks, the *bata scoir* which Irish-speaking children wore around their necks, as a crude disciplinary measure. National School teachers adopted the *bata scoir* to help them end the use of Irish: every time a child was heard speaking in Irish, a notch was cut in the stick; at the end of the day the notches were counted and the child punished for each offence.

There is a depressing fatalism about the *bata scoir*, used by Irish people themselves and not forced upon them by any official edict. The great native Irish cultural force embodied in the language was consciously thrust aside by the very people whose national identity and pride it had sustained for centuries. No doubt this was a symptom of their wretched, conquered state when they perceived survival as depending upon their ability to conform to the image of their conquerors and governors. It is when people lose confidence in themselves that extremism flourishes. In many ways, Patrick Pearse and his colleagues in 1916 represented the last generation which had a coherent sense of Irish language and culture. Even then, while admiring a legendary past and attempting to emulate the legendary Gael, English was their language: their rebel proclamation of an Irish republic in 1916 was printed and published only in English; the orders they gave their Irish Republican Army were in English; the letters and poems they wrote just before their executions were in English. Despite their rejection of the thought, their country had been Anglicized by a combination of education, social pressure and the famine.

Irish emigrants carried one other significant effect of the famine abroad: their hatred of Britain. Britain was blamed for the famine, and was the target of all their resentment. Irish emigrants to the

United States came to form a body of political opinion consistently hostile to British interests. In both world wars, American isolationism was strongly supported by Irish-Americans. Substantial financial and propaganda support has come from America for every Irish national movement from the nineteenth-century Home Rule Party to the IRA today. American politicians and presidents have found it prudent, for domestic political reasons, to use their influence on Britain in Irish interests. In 1919–20, Eamon de Valera, Ireland's nationalist political leader at the time, considered himself better employed in America where he raised over five million dollars in less than two years and tried to influence the 1920 American presidential election in the Irish interest. Presidents Woodrow Wilson and Warren G. Harding both exerted diplomatic pressure for an Irish settlement upon Lloyd George's government. It was from America, too, that the Irish Republican Brotherhood, the most effective of all Ireland's revolutionary national movements, was financed and sustained from the time of its foundation in 1858.

4

Ether Is Demonstrated as a Surgical Anesthetic: October 16, 1846

Anesthesia Permanently Altered Surgical Practice

by Martin S. Pernick

The use of ether as a surgical anesthetic was successfully demonstrated in public for the first time on October 16, 1846, at Massachusetts General Hospital in Boston. Local dentist William Morton administered inhaled sulfuric ether to a patient who then underwent surgical excision of a facial tumor. The goal was achieved: The patient felt no pain during the surgery. News of anesthesia's success quickly spread in the United States and in Europe.

Morton was not the first doctor to use ether successfully, but he was the first to conduct a public demonstration and his results were the first to be widely published. Only after Morton's demonstration did ether inhalation become the standard means of rendering patients insensitive to pain. Furthermore, the worldwide use of surgical ether marks the most rapid adoption of a medical innovation in the mid–nineteenth century. As a result, Morton is given most of the credit for introducing anesthesia into surgical practice despite the contributions of others to the technique.

In this article, Martin S. Pernick recounts Morton's first surgical ether demonstration. He also describes the swiftness with which news of the successful experiment spread. Pernick addresses the

Martin S. Pernick, *A Calculus of Suffering: Pain, Professionalism, and Anesthesia in Nineteenth-Century America*. New York: Columbia University Press, 1985. Copyright © 1985 by Columbia University Press, 61 W. 62nd St., New York, NY 10023. All rights reserved. Republished by permission.

controversy surrounding the new practice; not all surgeons began using ether inhalation as an anesthetic, and its administration was inconsistent. Pernick cites cultural reasons behind some doctors' choice not to engage in a medically accepted method of preventing pain.

Martin S. Pernick is professor of history at the University of Michigan in Ann Arbor. He is the author of several books on the history of medicine in the United States.

On October 16, 1846, a Boston dentist named William T.G. Morton first demonstrated that the vapor of sulphuric or diethyl ether could prevent the pain of surgery. In the steep-walled, bleacher-seated, domed amphitheater of the Massachusetts General Hospital, Morton administered his "Letheon Gas" to a young printer about to have a large tumor cut from his face. The operation, performed by Boston's preeminent surgeon, John Collins Warren, failed to fully remove the massive growth, but the ether succeeded in rendering the patient largely insensible to pain.

The Use of Anesthesia Spreads

Use of the new discovery spread with unprecedented speed. Within three months of Morton's demonstration, the leading hospitals of New York, London, and Paris began employing ether anesthesia. In Vienna, St. Petersburg, even far-off Canton, surgeons rapidly adopted the new discovery. By 1848, nitrous oxide (laughing gas), chloroform, and other compounds had been added to the list of known anesthetics. The new painkillers found employment in dentistry, obstetrics, and therapeutics, in addition to surgery. Some enthusiastic prophets predicted the imminent end of all human suffering.

The use of anesthesia spread far more rapidly than had such earlier innovations as smallpox vaccination or would such later discoveries as antisepsis. Vaccination remained controversial for over a century after Jenner's initial experiment [English physician Edward Jenner was the first to use the vaccination method in 1796]; antisepsis aroused bitter opposition for more than three decades following Lister's first demonstration [English surgeon Joseph Lister demonstrated the first use of antiseptics in surgery in 1865]. Anesthetics won acceptance at most major world medical institutions within a few months of Morton's exhibition. With the introduction of ether at the Pennsylvania Hospital in July 1853, the new discovery gained the approval of virtually the last of its opponents—all within seven years.

Yet the rapid diffusion of anesthetic use did *not* mean the end of painful surgery for all patients. There was, for example, a man named McGonigle, an immigrant laborer living in Philadelphia. On July 15, 1862, he fell while intoxicated, severely fracturing his ankle. He was rushed to the Pennsylvania Hospital, where his foot was immediately amputated. Although it was almost sixteen years after the discovery of anesthesia and nearly a decade after ether had been adopted at the Pennsylvania Hospital, McGonigle received no anesthetic at any time during the operation. Two days later, he died of shock.

McGonigle's case was not very unusual. Over the years 1853 to 1862, about 32 percent of all major limb amputations for fractures at the Pennsylvania Hospital took place on conscious patients. Even at the Massachusetts General Hospital, one of every three potentially painful operations in 1847 was performed without anesthesia. In the five years following their first use of ether, the surgeons of the New York Hospital may have done as many as one-third of their amputations on nonanesthetized people.

Private surgery seemingly followed the same pattern, though the statistical evidence is more limited. Most operations in antebellum America took place, not in hospitals, but in individual homes or medical offices. Unfortunately, without the discipline of institutional regulations, surgeons rarely kept detailed records of their private practices. One exception was Dr. Frank Hamilton of New York, a pioneer in the use of medical statistics, who kept case records covering his thirty-five years of experience as America's foremost expert on fractures. Hamilton first used ether in August 1847 and had tried chloroform by July 1849. Yet, over the next quarter century, more than one-sixth of the nonmilitary amputations he performed were done on conscious patients. In June 1873, for example, an anonymous twenty-three-year-old Irishman was run over by a railroad train in New York. Hamilton amputated the man's leg, without administering any anesthetic. Despite his gruesome ordeal, the patient recovered.

In addition to the available statistics, anecdotal accounts from a wide variety of sources confirm that instances of nonanesthetic surgery remained common occurrences long after most surgeons had adopted the use of anesthesia. Physicians and laypeople, easterners and westerners, in tones ranging from acceptance to outrage, recorded numerous cases of surgery without anesthesia performed in the 1850s and 1860s. As late as 1876, the respected *Cincinnati Lancet* published an article on "Alcohol as an Anaesthetic." The author advocated replacing chloroform with a stiff drink, in at least some cases of surgery, and reported three successful case histories. In short, many if not most mid-nineteenth-century practitioners who recorded their views or practices anesthetized some of their patients and not others. The issue for them was not whether to use anesthetics but when and on whom. . . .

Anesthesia as a Mixed Blessing

Even its most ardent advocates agreed anesthesia had drawbacks. Such criticisms derived from rational and humane concerns, including the belief that anesthesia could be dangerous, that pain could be valuable, that the power over others conferred by anesthesia could be abused, and that its use violated professional norms. And the alleged advantages were as varied as the drawbacks; they too included issues of power and status in addition to benevolence. The introduction of anesthesia was not a simple triumph of progress over reaction, humanitarianism over sadism. Most practitioners saw anesthesia as neither all good nor all bad but as a mixed blessing to be used selectively.

This discretionary nineteenth-century use of anesthesia drew upon a new utilitarian approach to professional decisionmaking, dubbed by its proponents "conservative medicine." "Conservative" doctrine cautioned that every drug had both good and bad effects; that the damage done by drugs and the damage done by disease were equally undesirable; and that professional duty required measuring the benefit-harm balance before employing any therapy. Conservative professionalism constituted a dramatic new departure in medical ethics, in its use of a utilitarian calculus to circumvent the ancient distinctions between acts of omission and of commission; between the effects of "Nature" and the results of human "Art." Medical conservatives adopted this approach in the hope it would provide a moderate synthesis, capable of reuniting a profession torn by scientific and ideological civil war.

Furthermore, conservative physicians held that their calculus of risks and benefits would vary widely from patient to patient. Thus nineteenth-century medical literature urged doctors to consider a patient's sex, race, age, ethnicity, economic class, personal habits, and temperament, as well as a wide range of technical factors, before using anesthetics. Women and children supposedly required painkillers more often than did men; the rich and educated more often than the poor and ignorant; etc. The operations considered too "minor" for anesthesia included many procedures that today are considered quite painful. And case statistics show that surgeons who kept records seemingly did follow the advice of this professional literature when actually prescribing anesthetics.

Anesthesia Changed Surgical Practice

Selective anesthetization often derived from the widely shared belief that different types of people differed in their sensitivity to pain, a doctrine whose implications reached far beyond anesthesia. The notion that women, children, whites, the rich, and the educated were more sensitive than were their social opposites played an important, previously unrecognized role in such diverse areas as feminism, imperialism, abolition, penology, pedagogy, and poetry. This tailoring of prescriptions to fit the patient, as well as the disease, provoked explicitly political controversy, because it required confronting the conflicting demands of individuality and equality.

Anesthetic usage spread more rapidly than any other medical innovation before the twentieth century. But whereas most physicians almost immediately adopted some uses of anesthesia, the frequency with which any given practitioner employed the new painkillers increased only gradually between 1846 and the 1870s. A doctor's age, sex, location, professional network, and therapeutic sect all influenced how often that physician prescribed anesthetics at any point in time; and the relationships sometimes proved surprising. Thus homeopaths and hydropaths, alternative healers who generally prided themselves on their mild, painless therapies, tended to employ anesthetics less frequently than did other, more orthodox practitioners.

By the 1880s a profusion of new anesthetic techniques, and a bacteriologically inspired revival of medical interventionism, marked the end of the era of selective anesthetization. Instead of choosing which patients were suitable for anesthesia, physicians could now select which anesthetic was best adapted to each operation. At the same time, new concepts of disease causality revolutionized both the technical and the ethical standards of surgical professionalism. But by then, anesthesia had already permanently changed both medicine and society.

Anesthesia deeply altered the practice of surgery. Case records indicate that, where anesthesia was introduced rapidly, it led to a dramatic increase in surgery; that these new operations were mostly necessary, not experimental; that the death rate following anesthetic surgery actually was much lower than most nineteenth-century physicians thought; and that industrialization, not anesthesia, caused the shocking midcentury increase in postoperative mortality. Anesthesia increased the power of surgeons over their patients; promoted the entry of women into surgery; fostered the bureaucratization of military and urban hospitals; and contributed to the "medicalization" of human suffering.

The *Communist Manifesto* Is Published:
January 1848

The *Manifesto's* History Reflects the Working-Class Movement

by Friedrich Engels

By the mid–nineteenth century, most of Europe had undergone the transition from an agricultural to an industrialized society. Agrarian and artisanal life waned as many people moved to cities to work in factories. This fundamental social shift was accompanied by the rise of the intellectual creeds known as socialism. Socialist thinkers and activists believed capitalism encouraged a powerful few to make more money at the expense of the working class and called for social equality to be achieved by transferring ownership of property and production to the government or the people collectively.

Karl Marx and Friedrich Engels were contributors to socialist philosophy. Their ideas differed from those of other thinkers in that they presented their claims as scientifically verifiable. They also rejected reform and instead called for revolution. Marx and Engels believed that history was determined by economics and class conflict. The social structure of capitalist society, they maintained, necessitated a radical transformation. The inevitable revolution would occur when the capitalist bourgeoisie (middle class) was overthrown by the industrial proletariat (working class). In this new Communist society, private property would be abolished. No group would oppress another group.

Friedrich Engels, "Preface," *Manifesto of the Communist Party*, by Karl Marx and Friedrich Engels, edited by Friedrich Engels. New York: International Publishers, 1996. Copyright © 1996 by International Publishers. Reproduced by permission.

At the request of German Communist League members working in London, Marx and Engels drafted a political program. The resulting pamphlet, the *Communist Manifesto*, appeared in January 1848. In time it became one of modern Europe's most influential political documents because of its importance in key movements such as the establishment of the Soviet Union in the early twentieth century.

Marx and Engels were well equipped to write the document; both were political writers by training and experience. In the years before 1848, Marx's pieces as a journalist and eventually as an editor promoted the abolition of private property and an insurrection of the working class. Engels was a contributor to a journal Marx coedited; the two became collaborators and wrote several works before publishing the *Communist Manifesto*.

In this selection, a preface written forty years after the *Communist Manifesto*'s original publication, Engels traces the history of the working-class movement since 1848. Developments across Europe in socialist thought and activism mirror the history of the *Manifesto* itself. That is, just as the Marx and Engels document has been published in many languages and cited as an influence on other thinkers, so, too, has the working-class movement spread to other nations and spawned movements in those countries.

The *Manifesto* was published as the platform of the Communist League, a workingmen's association, first exclusively German, later on international, and, under the political conditions of the [European] Continent before 1848, unavoidably a secret society. At a Congress of the League, held in London in November 1847, Marx and Engels were commissioned to prepare for publication a complete theoretical and practical party program. Drawn up in German, in January 1848, the manuscript was sent to the printer in London a few weeks before the French revolution of February 24th. A French translation was brought out in Paris, shortly before the insurrection of June 1848. The first English translation, by Miss Helen Macfarlane, appeared in George Julian Harney's *Red Republican*, London, 1850. A Danish and a Polish edition had also been published.

The defeat of the Parisian insurrection of June 1848—the first great battle between proletariat and bourgeoisie—drove again into the background, for a time, the social and political aspirations of the European working class. Thenceforth, the struggle for supremacy was again, as it had been before the revolution of February, solely between different sections of the propertied class; the working class was reduced to a fight for political elbow-room, and to the position of extreme wing of the middle-class Radicals. Wherever independent proletarian movements continued to show signs of life, they were ruthlessly hunted down. Thus the Prussian police hunted out the Central Board of the Communist League, then located in Cologne [in Germany.] The members were arrested, and, after eighteen months' imprisonment, they were tried in October 1852. This celebrated "Cologne Communist Trial" lasted from October 4th till November 12th; seven of the prisoners were sentenced to terms of imprisonment in a fortress, varying from three to six years. Immediately after the sentence, the League was formally dissolved by the remaining members. As to the *Manifesto*, it seemed thenceforth to be doomed to oblivion.

When the European working class had recovered sufficient strength for another attack on the ruling classes, the International Working-men's Association sprang up. But this association, formed with the express aim of welding into one body the whole militant proletariat of Europe and America, could not at once proclaim the principles laid down in the *Manifesto*. The International was bound to have a program broad enough to be acceptable to the English trade unions, to the followers of Proudhon [Pierre Joseph Proudhon (1809–1865), an anarchist, wrote works denouncing both industry and the dominance of government] in France, Belgium, Italy, and Spain, and to the Lassalleans [Ferdinand Lasalle (1825–1864) was a labor agitator who urged worker participation in German politics] in Germany. Marx, who drew up this program to the satisfaction of all parties, entirely trusted to the intellectual development of the working class, which was sure to result from combined action and mutual discussion. The very events and vicissitudes of the struggle against capital, the defeats even more than the victories, could not help bringing home to men's minds the insufficiency of their various favorite nostrums, and preparing the way for a more complete insight into the true conditions of working-class emancipation. And Marx was right. The International, on its breaking up in 1874, left the workers quite different men from what it had found them in 1864. Proudhonism in France, Lassalleanism in Germany were dying out, and even the conservative English trade unions, though most of them had long since severed their connection with the International, were gradually advancing towards that point at which, last year at Swansea, their president could say in their name "continental Socialism has lost its terrors for us." In fact, the principles of the *Manifesto* had made considerable headway among the workingmen of all countries.

The *Manifesto* itself thus came to the front again. Since 1850 the German text had been reprinted several times in Switzerland, England, and America. In 1872, it was translated into English in New York, where the translation was published in *Woodhull and Claflin's Weekly*. From this English version, a French one was made in *Le Socialiste* of New York. Since then at least two more English translations, more or less mutilated, have been brought out in America, and one of them has been reprinted in England. The first Russian translation, made by Bakunin [Mikhail Bakunin of Russia (1814–1876) was a radical anarchist who envisioned an international federation of autonomous communities], was published at Herzen's [Aleksander Herzen (1812–1870) was an influential radical philosopher and critic of Russian czarism] *Kolokol* office in Geneva, about 1863; a second one, by the heroic Vera Zasulich [Vera Zasulich (1849–1919) attempted to assassinate the military governor of St. Petersburg, Russia, in 1878], also in Geneva, in 1882. A new Danish edition is to be found in *Socialdemokratisk Bibliothek*, Copenhagen, 1885; a fresh French translation in *Le Socialiste*, Paris, 1886. From this latter, a Spanish version was prepared and published in Madrid, in 1886. Not counting the German reprints there had been at least twelve editions. An Armenian translation, which was to be published in Constantinople some months ago, did not see the light, I am told, because the publisher was afraid of bringing out a book with the name of Marx on it, while the translator declined to call it his own production. Of further translations into other languages I have heard, but have not seen. Thus the history of the *Manifesto* reflects, to a great extent, the history of the modern working-class movement; at present it is undoubtedly the most widespread, the most international production of all Socialist literature, the common platform acknowledged by millions of workingmen from Siberia to California.

Communist, Not Socialist

Yet, when it was written, we could not have called it a *Socialist* manifesto. By Socialists, in 1847, were understood, on the one hand, the adherents of the various Utopian systems: Owenites [Robert Owen (1771–1858) was a British Socialist who advocated "enlightened management"—the creation of a humane yet profitable industrial environment] in England, Fourierists [Charles Fourier (1772–1837) of France believed in agrarian socialism and community living constructed so as to avoid the boredom of industrial life] in France, both of them already reduced to the position of mere sects, and gradually dying out; on the other hand, the most multifarious social quacks, who, by all manners of tinkering, professed to redress, without any danger to capital and profit, all sorts of social grievances, in both cases men outside the working class movement, and looking rather to the "educated" classes for support. Whatever portion of the working class had become convinced of the insufficiency of mere political revolutions, and had proclaimed the necessity of a total social change, called itself Communist. It was a crude, rough-hewn, purely instinctive sort of Communism; still, it touched the cardinal point and was powerful enough amongst the working class to produce the Utopian Communism of Cabet in France, and of Weitling in Germany. Thus, in 1847, Socialism was a middle-class movement, Communism a working-class movement. Socialism was, on the continent at least, "respectable"; Communism was the very opposite. And as our notion, from the very beginning, was that "the emancipation of the working class must be the act of the working class itself," there could be no doubt as to which of the two names we must take. Moreover, we have, ever since, been far from repudiating it.

The *Manifesto* being our joint production, I consider myself bound to state that the fundamental proposition which forms its nucleus, belongs to Marx. That proposition is: That in every historical epoch, the prevailing mode of economic production and exchange, and the social organization necessarily following from it, form the basis upon which is built up, and from which alone can be explained, the political and intellectual history of that epoch; that consequently the whole history of mankind (since the dissolution of primitive tribal society, holding land in common ownership) has been a history of class struggles, contests between exploiting and exploited, ruling and oppressed classes; that the history of these class struggles form a series of evolutions in which, nowadays, a stage has been reached where the exploited and oppressed class—the proletariat—cannot attain its emancipation from the sway of the exploiting and ruling class—the bourgeoisie—without at the same time, and once and for all, emancipating society at large from all exploitation, oppression, class distinctions, and class struggles.

The Marxist Principle in History

This proposition, which, in my opinion, is destined to do for history what Darwin's theory has done for biology, we, both of us, had been gradually approaching for some years before 1845. How far I had independently progressed towards it, is best shown by my *Condition of the Working Class in England.* But when I again met Marx at Brussels, in spring 1845, he had it already worked out, and put it before me, in terms almost as clear as those in which I have stated it here.

From our joint preface to the German edition of 1872, I quote:

"However much the state of things may have altered during the last 25 years, the general principles laid down in this *Manifesto* are, on the whole, as correct today as ever. Here and there some detail might be improved. The practical application of the principles will depend, as the *Manifesto* itself states, everywhere and at all times, on the historical conditions for the time being existing, and, for that reason, no special stress is laid on the revolutionary measures proposed. . . . That passage would, in many respects, be very differently worded today. In view of the gigantic strides of modern industry since 1848, and of the accompanying improved and extended organization of the working class, in view of the practical experience gained, first in the February revolution, and then, still more, in the Paris Commune, where the proletariat for the first time held political power for two whole months, this program has in some details become antiquated. One thing especially was proved by the Commune, viz., that 'the working class cannot simply lay hold of the ready-made state machinery, and wield it for its own purposes.'. . . Further, it is self-evident, that the criticism of Socialist literature is deficient in relation to the present time, because it comes down only to 1847; also, that the remarks on the relation of the Communists to the various opposition parties . . . although in principle still correct, yet in practice are antiquated, because the political situation has been entirely changed, and the progress of history has swept from off the earth the greater portion of the political parties there enumerated.

"But then, the *Manifesto* has become a historical document which we have no longer any right to alter."

5 The *Communist Manifesto* Is Published: January 1848

Communists Support the Abolition of Private Property

by Karl Marx and Friedrich Engels

The *Communist Manifesto* of Karl Marx and Friedrich Engels, published as a pamphlet in January 1848, was a political plan of action. It was designed to address the problems of class conflict, perceived by the authors as an unwelcome by-product of industrialization. Marx and Engels explained history from an economic perspective: The capitalist bourgeoisie (wealthy middle class) and the proletariat (the working class) inevitably will clash, culminating in a new society in which class conflict will end. The authors claimed that these economic "laws" both had a scientific basis and determined the course of history.

Marx and Engels outlined a number of features of their Communist society. These included the abolition of private property and rights of inheritance as well as the nationalization of banks, factories, transportation, communication, and land. The *Manifesto* also advocated a graduated income tax, laws requiring all to work (though abolishing child labor), and free public schools. They believed that achieving this change required not simply reform, but revolution. Only when the working class rises up to overthrow the bourgeoisie, they argue, will the new, classless society be born.

Karl Marx and Friedrich Engels, *Manifesto of the Communist Party*, edited by Friedrich Engels. New York: International Publishers, 1996. Copyright © 1996 by International Publishers. Reproduced by permission.

In the following excerpt, the authors compare the Communists with other working-class parties. Marx and Engels explain Communist theory and the reasons why abolition of private property is central to their program.

I n what relation do the Communists stand to the proletarians as a whole?

The Communists do not form a separate party opposed to other working-class parties.

They have no interests separate and apart from those of the proletariat as a whole.

They do not set up any sectarian principles of their own, by which to shape and mould the proletarian movement.

The Communists and Other Working-Class Parties

The Communists are distinguished from the other working-class parties by this only: 1. In the national struggles of the proletarians of the different countries, they point out and bring to the front the common interests of the entire proletariat, independently of all nationality. 2. In the various stages of development which the struggle of the working class against the bourgeoisie has to pass through, they always and everywhere represent the interests of the movement as a whole.

The Communists, therefore, are on the one hand, practically, the most advanced and resolute section of the working-class parties of every country, that section which pushes forward all others; on the other hand, theoretically, they have over the great mass of the proletariat the advantage of clearly understanding the line of march, the conditions, and the ultimate general results of the proletarian movement.

The immediate aim of the Communists is the same as that of all the other proletarian parties: Formation of the proletariat into a class, overthrow of bourgeois supremacy, conquest of political power by the proletariat.

The theoretical conclusions of the Communists are in no way based on ideas or principles that have been invented, or discovered, by this or that would-be universal reformer.

They merely express, in general terms, actual relations springing from an existing class struggle, from a historical movement going on under our very eyes. The abolition of existing property relations is not at all a distinctive feature of Communism.

All property relations in the past have continually been subject to historical change consequent upon the change in historical conditions.

The French Revolution, for example, abolished feudal property in favor of bourgeois property.

The distinguishing feature of Communism is not the abolition of property generally, but the abolition of bourgeois property. But modern bourgeois private property is the final and most complete expression of the system of producing and appropriating products that is based on class antagonisms, on the exploitation of the many by the few.

In this sense, the theory of the Communists may be summed up in the single sentence: Abolition of private property.

Abolishing Private Property

We Communists have been reproached with the desire of abolishing the right of personally acquiring property as the fruit of a man's own labor, which property is alleged to be the groundwork of all personal freedom, activity, and independence.

Hard-won, self-acquired, self-earned property! Do you mean the property of the petty artisan and of the small peasant, a form of property that preceded the bourgeois form? There is no need to abolish that; the development of industry has to a great extent already destroyed it, and is still destroying it daily.

Or do you mean modern bourgeois private property?

But does wage-labor create any property for the laborer? Not a bit. It creates capital, i.e., that kind of property which exploits wage-labor, and which cannot increase except upon condition of begetting a new supply of wage-labor for fresh exploitation. Property, in its present form, is based on the antagonism of capital and wage-labor. Let us examine both sides of this antagonism.

To be a capitalist, is to have not only a purely personal, but a social *status* in production. Capital is a collective product, and only by the united action of many members, nay, in the last resort, only by the united action of all members of society, can it be set in motion.

Capital is therefore not a personal, it is a social, power.

When, therefore, capital is converted into common property, into the property of all members of society, personal property is not thereby transformed into social property. It is only the social character of the property that is changed. It loses its class character.

Let us now take wage-labor.

The average price of wage-labor, is the minimum wage, i.e., that quantum of the means of subsistence which is absolutely requisite to keep the laborer in bare existence as a laborer. What, therefore, the wage-laborer appropriates by means of his labor, merely suffices to prolong and reproduce a bare existence. We by no means intend to abolish this personal appropriation of the products of labor, an appropriation that is made for the maintenance and reproduction of human life, and that leaves no surplus wherewith to command the labor of others. All that we want to do away with is the miserable character of this appropriation, under which the laborer lives merely to increase capital, and is allowed to live only insofar as the interest of the ruling class requires it.

In bourgeois society, living labor is but a means to increase accumulated labor. In Communist society, accumulated labor is but a means to widen, to enrich, to promote the existence of the laborer.

The Present Dominates the Past

In bourgeois society, therefore, the past dominates the present; in Communist society, the present dominates the past. In bourgeois society capital is independent and has individuality, while the living person is dependent and has no individuality.

And the abolition of this state of things is called by the bourgeois, abolition of individuality and freedom! And rightly so. The abolition of bourgeois individuality, bourgeois independence, and bourgeois freedom is undoubtedly aimed at.

By freedom is meant, under the present bourgeois conditions of production, free trade, free selling and buying.

But if selling and buying disappears, free selling and buying disappears also. This talk about free selling and buying, and all the other "brave words" of our bourgeoisie about freedom in general, have a meaning, if any, only in contrast with restricted selling and buying, with the fettered traders of the Middle Ages, but have no meaning when opposed to the Communist abolition of buying and selling, of the bourgeois conditions of production, and of the bourgeoisie itself.

You are horrified at our intending to do away with private property. But in your existing society, private property is already done away with for nine-tenths of the population; its existence for the few is solely due to its non-existence in the hands of those nine-tenths. You reproach us, therefore, with intending to do away with a form of property, the necessary condition for whose existence is the nonexistence of any property for the immense majority of society.

In a word, you reproach us with intending to do away with your property. Precisely so; that is just what we intend.

From the moment when labor can no longer be converted into capital, money, or rent, into a social power capable of being monopolized, i.e., from the moment when individual property can no longer be transformed into bourgeois property, into capital, from that moment, you say, individuality vanishes.

You must, therefore, confess that by "individual" you mean no other person than the bourgeois, than the middle-class owner of property. This person must, indeed, be swept out of the way, and made impossible.

Communism deprives no man of the power to appropriate the products of society; all that it does is to deprive him of the power to subjugate the labor of others by means of such appropriation.

It has been objected, that upon the abolition of private property all work will cease, and universal laziness will overtake us.

According to this, bourgeois society ought long ago to have gone to the dogs through sheer idleness; for those of its members who work, acquire nothing, and those who acquire anything, do not work. The whole of this objection is but another expression of the tautology: There can no longer be any wage-labor when there is no longer any capital.

All objections urged against the Communist mode of producing and appropriating material products, have, in the same way, been urged against the Communist modes of producing and appropriating intellectual products. Just as, to the bourgeois, the disappearance of class property is the disappearance of production itself, so the disappearance of class culture is to him identical with the disappearance of all culture.

That culture, the loss of which he laments, is, for the enormous majority, a mere training to act as a machine.

But don't wrangle with us so long as you apply, to our intended abolition of bourgeois property, the standard of your bourgeois notions of freedom, culture, law, etc. Your very ideas are but the outgrowth of the conditions of your bourgeois production and bourgeois property, just as your jurisprudence is but the will of your class made into a law for all, a will whose essential character and direction are determined by the economic conditions of existence of your class.

The selfish misconception that induces you to transform into eternal laws of nature and of reason, the social forms springing from your present mode of production and form of property—historical relations that rise and disappear in the progress of production—this misconception you share with every ruling class that has preceded you. What you see clearly in the case of ancient property, what you admit in the case of feudal property, you are of course forbidden to admit in the case of your own bourgeois form of property.

The Revolutions of 1848 Changed European Politics

by Peter N. Stearns

The revolutions that swept Europe in 1848 are a political hallmark of the nineteenth century. The first revolt broke out in France. On February 22, 1848, the French government banned a demonstration in favor of electoral reform. Popular protest erupted immediately, culminating in King Louis-Philippe's abdication two days later. The revolutionary spirit in France set off a chain reaction; throughout the course of 1848, nearly every European country and empire except for Spain and Russia was touched by rebellion.

Three factors contributed to the revolutionary climate in 1848. The first was a two-year economic crisis that caused unemployment and high prices throughout Europe. The second was the transition to an industrial society that alienated some segments of the workforce and led to discontent. Third was residual unrest from unsuccessful previous uprisings.

In the following selection, Peter N. Stearns explains the importance of the 1848 revolutions in nineteenth-century European history. Though the phenomenon affected the whole continent, Stearns points out that events and outcomes differed in each nation. France, for example, was a developed country that had withstood several revolutions. Hungary, by contrast, was new both to the revolutionary experience and to that of national development. Thus context and causes varied widely. Sterns does point to a significant common

Peter N. Stearns, *1848: The Revolutionary Tide in Europe.* New York: W.W. Norton, 1974. Copyright © 1974 by Peter N. Stearns. All rights reserved. Reproduced by permission.

outcome, however: None of the countries that underwent revolution in 1848 has since experienced another revolution except in the aftermath of war.

Historian Peter N. Stearns is a prolific author specializing in American and European social and cultural history. He is presently the provost of George Mason University in Fairfax, Virginia.

The Revolutionary Outburst of 1848 was unprecedented in Europe. Two centuries before to the very year, revolts had developed in southern Italy, Spain, and Muscovy, while Leveller agitation crested in Britain and the Fronde rebellion shook France. These revolts had some common features with those of 1848, including a severe famine in the two preceding years, but they were not the result of direct revolutionary contagion and for the most part their impact was muted. Revolutionary change had spread widely in Western and Central Europe after the French Revolution of 1789, but, except in France, this was due mainly to the conquests of French armies, not to a series of rebellions. More recently still, 1830 had proved a foretaste of the revolutionary current. Revolt in France was followed by outbreaks in Belgium, Poland, and central Italy, while agitation mounted in Germany and Britain. But only in 1848 did revolution assume virtually continental proportions. Russia and Spain were exempt, of the larger countries. Serious revolutions broke out in France, Italy, German, Austria, Bohemia, and Hungary, while there were stirrings of some significance in Switzerland, Denmark, Rumania, Poland, and Ireland. Britain, although apparently immune to formal revolution, saw the last wave of Chartist agitation, And for the most part these various risings were interconnected, linked by economic causation, ideology, and by the fascination of revolution itself. Knowledge that a regime elsewhere had been shaken seemed a valid reason to try the same thing in one's own backyard.

An Event with Few Parallels

This was a special moment, for the revolutionary current has never been so strong in Europe since that time. Indeed this kind of contagion has few parallels anywhere in world history. There have been some peak revolutionary years since World War II in the developing nations—1958 in parts of the Near East and Asia, for example. These offer some interesting analogies with 1848 in Europe, where most of the countries involved in revolution were undergoing the stress of mounting industrialization and commercialization and where nationalism was spreading to many new areas. Clearly, a special combination of factors is required for revolution to flow so easily across state boundaries, without being imported by force of arms.

Of course each separate revolution in 1848 had its own character. The "stirrings" must be distinguished from the real revolts. Nationalist intellectuals and professional people had a week of agitation in Ireland, but they could not rouse the masses and could not contend with clever British repression. The effort does not loom large in the history of Irish protest. The Rumanian revolt also failed to catch fire, for here the masses were not roused by nationalism and found no other issues. But the attempt by agitators drawn from the small middle class and elements of the aristocracy fed further discontent and helped prepare the formation of the Rumanian nation a decade later. Chartist protest in Britain completely failed to make a revolution. In this case large segments of the lower classes did stir, but they lacked any cooperation from above; and they were divided among themselves and few of them were consciously revolutionary.

Different Countries, Different Revolution

In France the revolution was above all an effort to complete the work of the radical phase of the great French Revolution to create a new, more open political regime. The most articulate revolutionary leaders sought a democratic republic that would guarantee key liberties to all citizens and that would enact some humanitarian reforms without destroying the social order. In this sense the revolution was far less fundamental than its predecessor, which had to overturn an older social structure in addition to battling for political change. The legal basis of the old regime was already gone, with the establishment of substantial equality under the laws and the abolition of the legal privileges of church and aristocracy. The revolution of 1830 still had anti-aristocratic overtones, and despite its mildness did succeed in chasing the more obdurate aristocrats and churchmen from power. 1848 had no such obvious targets. It sought to juggle the holders of power, not to overturn the basic structure. It is therefore much less important in French history than the revolution of 1789, much less important in European history than many of the risings it induced elsewhere in 1848–1849.

Yet France was the most advanced country in which revolution did occur in those years, not only politically but also economically and socially. Industrialization was more extensive than in Central Europe. The major social classes were better defined and were involved, willy-nilly, in more new ways of doing things. It is not surprising, then, that beneath the surface of the revolution an array of movements and ideas took shape that had quite a modern ring. Some of these came to the fore during the revolution itself. The June Days of 1848, which so cruelly ended the political thrust of the revolution, were in part the repetition of traditional battles between the urban poor and the established order, but they had elements of more modern class warfare as well. Other protest currents, such as feminism, did not play a major role in the revolution itself, but were given a significant boost. In France more than elsewhere, we might say that the revolution of 1848 put items on the agenda for the next great surge of protest, in which we are to a great extent still engaged.

At the other extreme was Hungary, where the revolution was really a new round of conflict between the local aristocracy and the Habsburg government. The Magyar aristocracy was unusually large and included many people who were quite poor; it harbored some social tensions that set class against class in other countries. But at least locally it was a ruling class, fighting to retain or revive its privileges. It used a rhetoric that resembled that of revolutions elsewhere. Liberalism and nationalism, sincerely advocated by leaders such as Lajos Kossuth, were useful additions to the arsenal of the aristocrats. The revolution itself proved how they could be disfigured in the interests of an older order. The revolution was profoundly important in Hungarian history. It set the tone for further strivings for a Hungarian state and for bitter ethnic and class tensions within that state, once achieved. But it differed most from the risings that developed elsewhere in the same years. This was an area barely touched by new social and economic currents, an agrarian country in which new ideas inevitably found a distinctive, and often limited, reception.

Important Revolutions in Central Europe

The revolutions in Central Europe proper, in Austria and particularly in the German states, were the most important of the lot. They challenged the existing diplomatic structure, in the name of nationalism. They sought a new political structure as well, and along with this, at least implicitly, a new social order. For these areas had had no great revolution like the French. The old regime still predominated. It had introduced some reforms, at least in the German states, which is one reason the revolutionaries lacked the zeal of their French counterparts a half century before. But this was the Germans' chance to make a new society, and they failed. They caused important changes, directly or indirectly. For some key groups, such as the peasants in many areas, a real revolution did occur at least in law. But the revolutions left enough of the old order intact to insure that only further revolution could create a liberal society. Yet they so disillusioned most revolutionaries that they made renewed revolt most improbable. Some historians have traced the whole of German history, through Hitler at least, to the failures of 1848. Others have found these failures themselves inevitable, because of fatal flaws in the German political character. Even for those who take a less deterministic view, it is clear that analysis of the causes and results of the German and Austrian revolutions is fundamental to an understanding of the modern history of Central Europe.

The Italian revolution, though similar to the German in many ways, has something of its own style. Part of the difference is subjective, because of the later histories of the two countries. The revolution was profoundly important in Italian history. Even more than in Germany it encouraged forces of nationalism that would triumph within a generation. As in Germany, liberalism failed in the revolutions; when it revived it was far more circumspect, even corruptible, than before. But none of this seems to matter as much in Italy, because Italy played a less villainous or at least less importantly villainous a role in European history thereafter. Hence historians have bemoaned the fate of the Italian revolutions less loudly, and outside of Italy they have analyzed it less extensively. Yet it is also true that while liberals were actively engaged in the Italian revolution, liberalism was less prominent than in Germany and Austria. Local risings, in Rome and in Venice, attacked the old regime directly. Indeed the Roman revolutionaries sought to go farther than any revolutionary regime of the period, seeking social as well as political change: but except in Rome and briefly in Sicily, the Italian revolutions did not take place in the most backward areas of Italy, where the regimes surpassed that of the Habsburg empire in their devotion to an unenlightened traditionalism leavened by police repression. And most of the revolutionaries did not focus on internal political change. They wanted it and they assumed it would come, but there was a more obvious enemy in the foreign—Austrian—domination that blanketed most of northern Italy. Much of the Italian revolution was thus a war of liberation, not a revolution at all. Though no less significant to subsequent national history, it was less complex than the German risings and it left the country's political future more open-ended. Italian liberalism undeniably changed as a result of the revolution, but it still seemed the wave of the future. Hence Piedmont, the ultimate leader of unification, began to assume a more liberal guise in the 1850s, while Prussia was on the whole confirmed in its conservatism even as it created a new Germany.

Generalizations Do Not Apply

So much for the national nutshells. It is obvious that any generalization about the revolutions of 1848 must be seriously qualified for each key area. Each revolution must be assessed in its own context, each had a distinctive impact. The revolutions spread from one point to another. They interacted to a limited extent. Even within the Habsburg empire where they theoretically faced a common foe in the existing regime, the major centers of revolution had little to do with each other. The drama of each revolution unfolded separately. Each had its own heroes, its own crises. Each therefore demands its own narrative. Almost all the existing histories of the revolution, and there are a number of good ones, understandably proceed on a case-by-case basis, with at most a few general remarks.

Yet the revolutions had more in common than their date. If no generalization covers the whole situation, there is significance to "the revolutions" that transcends each particular situation. Else why write a history of the revolutions, instead of a single one that strikes the fancy, much less read one?

The collective impact of the revolutions shattered the diplomatic framework of Europe that had been created by the Congress of Vienna. The results were delayed, to be sure, surfacing clearly only after 1856 with the Crimean War settlement and the split among the conservative powers. But even before that it was obvious the revolution had opened new horizons to existing states. The King of Prussia began to think about a federated Germany with himself at its head. Piedmont began to prepare for aggrandizement, though defeated during the revolution itself. France elected a president vowed to remake the European map. This was not the main reason for his election, but there was little question that the revolutionary forces in France were tired of the nation's passive attitude and eager for a policy that would at once liberate other areas from conservative regimes and add to France's glory—the classic formula of revolutionary French nationalism. Nationalists elsewhere, seeking to create new states, failed in their immediate efforts but learned from their failure. Even as they worked for their own nation alone, they contributed to a general and fundamental reordering of European diplomacy.

Successes and Problems of the Revolutions

Yet, if this is the most obvious common element of the revolutions, it is not the most important one. Almost everywhere the revolutions flowed from similar forces, both social and ideological. Almost everywhere they foundered on common problems, including severe tensions among the social groups that made them and important contradictions within their ideological base.

The failure of the revolutions must be assessed with care. None failed completely. All unleashed or encouraged forces that would win still greater victories, though without revolution and with important limitations, within a generation. Yet nowhere save perhaps in Switzerland were the revolutions really successful in achieving their professed goals. Hence, to the multiplicity of revolutions must be added their quick defeat. This makes it difficult to analyze them in terms of any model of revolution. We can analyze characteristics derived from knowledge of great revolutions, like the Russian or the French, to assess these revolts and help explain their collapse; in this sense they may help test existing models. But they went through few of the classic stages of a successful revolution. It can plausibly be argued, in fact, that they were not really revolutions at all, in that in most instances they did not provide an alternate political and military structure and in many the revolutionary leaders did not even want to do so. Why, then, bother with them?

In the first place, the revolutions ended an era. With the revolutions the age of romanticism drew to a close. Heirs of the romantic tradition continued their work—they continue it still. But romanticism's dominance in the realm of ideas was over, and so was the confidence of romantics themselves that they could remake the world in their image. More basically the revolutions signaled a change in the relationship between intellectuals and society. It seemed natural for intellectuals to assume leadership of the revolutions, although in fact they had never wielded such broad powers before. They had, after all, spearheaded most of the political movements that fed the revolutions. Their role was assuredly not exhausted by the revolutions, but never again, in Western and Central Europe, could they assume command. Changes in their own outlook and in the nature of political organization, both of which the revolutions furthered, reduced their prestige.

1848 Ended the Age of Revolutions

Above all, the revolutions of 1848 ended the age of revolutions that had begun in the eighteenth century. None of the countries involved in the 1848 risings, except Hungary, has ever again experienced revolution save as the aftermath of defeat in war, and even in Hungary's case the 1956 rising was indirectly the product of loss in war. The revolutions of 1848 played a major role in this dramatic change. Because of them, established governments learned better how to maintain order. They improved their ability both to repress and to conciliate. Key groups that had supported revolutions for almost a century, such as many peasants and artisans, either won their major demands or lost their nerve as a result of their failure. More basic processes were at work, to be sure. Artisans were losing ground in an industrializing society. Improvements in the regularity of food supplies after midcentury removed one of the classic grievances of the lower classes. Nevertheless the revolutions stand as the last major traditional protest by the masses in Western and Central Europe and the last major effort directly to block the spread of industrialization itself. Along with the decline of revolution in the most economically advanced sections of Europe came a more general change in the nature and purpose of protest. The dimensions of this change began to emerge in the later stages of the revolutions themselves.

All of which is to say that revolutions were not only an end but a beginning. Many of the positive goals of the articulate revolutionaries pointed the way to a new age. Nationalism, liberalism, socialism—most of the basic political forces that are with us today were changed and enhanced by the revolutions. Nationalism was undoubtedly the biggest gainer. A minor, sputtering movement before the revolutions, it won new currency despite the formal failure of the nationalist goals. But all the new political movements earned new attention and their proponents learned new, often more effective means of organization. The transition from utopian socialism to Marxism, for example, was immeasurably furthered by the lessons of the revolutions.

The results of 1848 encouraged the articulation of a modern class structure. The middle classes were placed on the side of the established order, because of the gains they won but even more because of the new fears they acquired. New lower-class groups, notably many factory workers, were drawn into protest during the course of the revolutions and the lower classes generally began to veer away from traditional demands as they developed a more modern political sense. These changes were only beginning. We must not expect to see, at the revolutions' end, a militant factory proletariat facing a terrorized bourgeoisie. The revolutions did, nevertheless, tend to further a new kind of social polarization.

In what they ended and in what they began, the principal revolutions of 1848 served as a transition from an old society to a new one. They captured the growing pains of areas on the verge of industrialization. In this, as much as in their specific achievements and failures, lies their fascination. In this lies also their contribution to an understanding of other societies, even in the present day, which are in a similar situation. Most of the participants in the revolutions sought to protest change, to return to older ways. They lost, even as conservative governments seemed to win the day. The revolutions opened the way to further change as they forced governments to adopt new methods to stay in power and as they helped reshape the mentality of large groups within the society at large. The revolutions, the result of a precarious balance between old and new, tipped the scales.

Polk Waged an Unjust War of Aggression

by William Dusinberre

Throughout the nineteenth century, the United States acquired territory through westward expansion. One of the most hotly disputed territories was Texas, a Mexican province that declared independence in 1836. Mexico did not fully recognize Texan independence, and broke off diplomatic relations when the United States annexed Texas in 1845. Territorial disputes continued, and the two nations went to war on May 13, 1846.

The U.S. president who oversaw the war effort was Democrat James K. Polk (1795–1849). The Democratic Party platform during Polk's 1844 campaign was expansionist in outlook: The party supported the annexation of Texas and the acquisition of Oregon. The U.S.-Mexican war ended with the Treaty of Guadalupe Hidalgo on May 30, 1848. Among its provisions were the recognition of the Rio Grande as the southern Texan border, as well as the cession of Texas and other territories constituting the present-day American southwest and California.

This selection by historian William Dusinberre recounts the origins of the Mexican War as well as its domestic consequences. Dusinberre criticizes Polk's foreign policy maneuver, accusing Polk of a bald grab for territory and linking the president's expansionist vision and policies to ensuing political strife in the 1850s and 1860s.

Historian William Dusinberre is Emeritus Reader at the Univer-

William Dusinberre, *Slavemaster President: The Double Career of James Polk*. New York: Oxford University Press, 2003.

sity of Warwick in England. He is the author of two books on slavery in America.

T he annexation of Texas, the Mexican War, and the subsequent political battle over slavery in the conquered territory are often examined separately. This is certainly how [President James K.] Polk sought to present these events. Yet, because the three issues were intimately interwoven, they cannot be properly viewed unless the interrelations among them are constantly held in mind.

Border Disputes Provoked Mexico

When Polk annexed Texas, he adopted the Texans' claims to the Rio Grande as their boundary, not only for their southern boundary but for their western border too. Texas had a sound claim to the Nueces River as its southern boundary, some 150 arid miles short of the Rio Grande, and it might perhaps have plausibly claimed even the watershed between the Nueces and the Rio Grande. Also, Texas might have reasonably claimed as its western border a line running from the headwaters of the Nueces River north and northwestward, or even a line from the watershed between the Nueces and the Rio Grande to the southeast corner of present-day New Mexico and thence straight north. This last line would have run some 200 miles east of the Rio Grande, as that river flows from the Rocky Mountains of Colorado almost due south through New Mexico to El Paso. The Texans, by extending their appetite westward to the Rio Grande, thus sought to devour more than half of the present state of New Mexico, including Santa Fe, Albuquerque, and Taos, to which they had no remotely legitimate claim. And on their southern border, the Texans' demand for the Rio Grande encompassed Mexican posts at Santiago and Laredo and settlements north of Matamoros, to which again Texas had no legitimate claim. Even the historian Justin Smith—a vigorous defender of the Mexican War—acknowledged (in a footnote) that he regarded the Texans' boundary "claim and all conclusions based upon it as unsound." And Polk's secretary of state, James Buchanan, had declared in 1844 that Texas's claim "to that portion of New Mexico which lies east of [the Rio Grande], and north of [El Paso], is certainly of a very doubtful character; and it is one upon which we ought not to insist." Polk did insist. He need not have adopted the

Texans' grandiose border claims, but he did so. These claims—increasing the assurance that Mexico would strenuously resent the annexation of Texas by the United States—furnished Polk the provocation that led in 1846 to war with Mexico, and the war enabled the United States to conquer a vast western domain, including California.

Even if Texas had been annexed with reasonable boundaries, war with Mexico might possibly have ensued, for the Mexican government had never offered to recognize Texan independence until May 1845, after the United States had proposed to annex Texas; and Mexico was even less happy at the idea of Texas's joining the United States. But Mexico would probably have swallowed its unhappiness—and avoided war—if the United States had not demanded the Rio Grande boundary. To Mexico, Polk's demand for the Rio Grande boundary was (1) a claim to take over long-established Mexican communities at and near Santa Fe; (2) a humiliating grab for the large, though unfertile, portion of the province of Coahuila, lying between the Rio Grande and the Nueces River, even though the Nueces had always (before the Texan claim of 1836) been accepted as the border between Texas and Coahuila; and (3) an American assertion of the right to aim artillery at what was by far the largest town in the whole region, Matamoros, situated on the south bank of the Rio Grande. Many Mexican military and civilian leaders were very reluctant to enter into a war with the United States, which they feared Mexico could not win. Because of this reluctance, Texas could probably have been annexed without war if the United States had not insisted on the Rio Grande as the boundary. A principal difference between Polk and the Whig Henry Clay—Polk's opponent in the presidential election of 1844—had been that Clay favored annexing Texas in some cautious way that would not precipitate military conflict. If Clay had won the election he certainly would not have demanded the Rio Grande as Texas's border.

President Polk insisted on the Rio Grande. He then ordered General Zachary Taylor to encamp his army "on or near the Rio Grande" in order to establish the claim. Taylor planted his troops in disputed territory just south of the Nueces River, although he cautiously held them back 150 miles from the Rio Grande, and Mexican authorities were reluctant to respond to this limited provocation. Polk repeatedly—on October 16, 1845, and January 13, 1846—urged Taylor to place his army "as near [the Rio

Grande] as circumstances will permit," but Taylor delayed moving until early March, and his troops did not reach the Rio Grande until March 28, 1846. No Mexican attack being immediately forthcoming, the impatient Polk, with the acquiescence of his cabinet, decided to ask Congress to declare war on Mexico. But before he actually sent his war message to Congress, Polk learned—fortunately, from his point of view—that a Mexican force had finally crossed the Rio Grande to ambush some of the recently arrived American soldiers. Polk was therefore able to redesign his war proposal: he alleged that war already existed "by the act of Mexico herself." Congress need not declare war at all but merely "recognize the existence of the war" already started by the enemy. . . .

It was a disgraceful episode. Rational consideration of whether or not to go to war for an "indefensible" border claim was swept aside. A president whose political career was founded on strict observance of the Constitution played fast and loose with proper par-

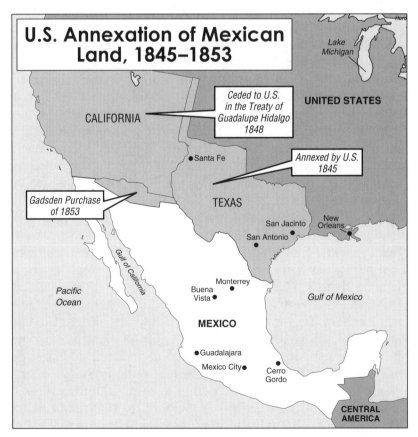

U.S. Annexation of Mexican Land, 1845–1853

liamentary procedure. He seemed to appeal to constitutional restraint only when it suited him to do so. And by whipping the war resolution through the House against the wishes of 35 percent of its members, the president planted the seeds of a towering political conflict over war aims: was slavery to be legalized in the territory Polk wished to seize from Mexico?

Territorial War Aims

Polk's subsequent policy toward Mexico was consistent with his opening salvo. The war was scarcely launched before the president told the cabinet he hoped to acquire all of Mexico north of the twenty-sixth parallel—not only New Mexico and California (which then contained present-day Arizona, Nevada, Utah, and parts of Colorado and Wyoming) but also another 300,000 square miles of Mexican territory, including most of the present-day Mexican states of Nuevo Leon, Coahuila, Chihuahua, Sonora, and Baja California. Once General Taylor had won a few battles in northern Mexico, Polk began to think that his grandiose territorial aspirations might be realized. "You need not be surprised," the president wrote his brother in October 1846, "if other Provinces [besides California and New Mexico] also are secured. . . . The longer the war . . . the greater will be . . . the indemnity required." (A few months later, Mexican authorities somehow got wind of Polk's appetite for the twenty-sixth parallel. Mexican nationalists then used allegations of Yankee land hunger to repel an unofficial American peace overture tendered early in 1847.)

Normally, Polk's military and diplomatic tactics were incremental. He applied military pressure first, thereafter making a demand on Mexico that no Mexican government would be likely to accept. Then, when his demand was not met, he applied additional military force and committed his negotiators to a new, more ambitious goal, which again the Mexican government—sometimes to Polk's surprise—would also be unwilling to accept; and the process was repeated. Thus Polk began by ordering General Taylor's army to the Rio Grande. While Taylor was still encamped at Corpus Christi (just south of the Nueces River), Mexico indicated willingness to talk to a special American commissioner, presumably about whether they might accept their loss of Texas to the United States in return for an American payment (such as had previously been paid to France for the Louisiana Purchase). Polk—regarding the annexation of Texas, without any cash payment to

Mexico, as a nonnegotiable fait accompli ["accomplished fact" (French)]—declined to discuss this issue, as the Mexicans seemed to have offered to do. Instead he appointed a "minister plenipo-tentiary"—not the ad hoc commissioner whom the Mexicans had requested—and instructed him to offer $5 million for the remain-der of New Mexico *west* of the Rio Grande; the agent was to of-fer up to $20 million more for parts of California.

When Mexico, predictably, declined to negotiate on these terms, Polk threatened war; he also posted the American navy to the Mexican port of Veracruz (ready to cut off the tariff revenues on which the Mexican government relied to pay its soldiers); and he sent General Taylor specific authorization to occupy the north bank of the Rio Grande, directly opposite the Mexican town of Matamoros. At that time Matamoros was much the largest town in the whole region. Its population of 15,000 was triple that of ei-ther Houston or Galveston (the largest towns in Texas). Taylor's encampment within artillery range of this important urban center led, predictably, to the Mexican ambush, which then covered Polk's (previously determined) decision to go to war.

Mexico Is Reluctant to Submit

Taylor's subsequent victories in northern Mexico during the next few months failed to produce the expected Mexican submission, whereupon Polk resolved to carry the war to central Mexico. His cabinet, however, was reluctant to extend military operations to-ward Mexico City. Once again, therefore, Polk employed incre-mental tactics: in November 1846 he got the cabinet to agree at least to a landing at Veracruz. In practice, this was sure to result in the desired military campaign toward Mexico City (for no in-vading American army was likely to sit passively on the pestilen-tial coast near Veracruz during the long summer of 1847, watch-ing its soldiers die of malaria and yellow fever, when a campaign into the mountains would offer respite from these scourges). Thus, by proceeding one step at a time, Polk eventually secured his cab-inet's assent to the campaign toward Mexico City.

Once General Winfield Scott's army had captured Veracruz—and with the prospect of Scott's march inland—Polk formulated instructions for a new diplomatic agent, Nicholas Trist. Before launching the war, Polk had set his minimum demand as, in effect, Mexican submission to the virtually uncompensated loss of Texas, but now the president's minimum demand was far more ambitious. He presented Mexico with the ultimatum to cede California and New Mexico, for which the United States would pay up to $20 million (and would waive various financial claims against Mexico), or the war would continue. Trist should also attempt to purchase Baja California (the long peninsula stretching 800 miles southward from San Diego) and to secure American transit rights from the Gulf of Mexico across the Isthmus of Tehuantepec (350 miles southeast of Mexico City) to the Pacific Ocean.

Five months later the Mexican government still refused to submit to the ultimatum, even though Scott's army had smashed the defenses of Mexico City and was poised to occupy the city itself. When news of this refusal reached Washington, Polk ordered Trist to break off contact with the Mexicans and return home, and the president once again put incremental tactics into service. A movement had developed in the United States to keep permanent possession of substantial portions of present-day Mexico. The two most important members of Polk's cabinet favored this policy. Secretary of State James Buchanan—a Pennsylvanian seeking the support of expansionists for the Democratic presidential nomination in 1848—wanted to keep the northeastern part of present-day Mexico, between the Gulf of Mexico and the Sierra Madre. Secretary of the Treasury Robert Walker (a Mississippian) hoped, like some other Democrats, to annex *all* of Mexico. Polk himself had envisaged, almost from the beginning of the war, seizing (besides California and New Mexico) most of the five other northern states of Mexico. Thus when the president told his cabinet in October 1847 that he favored further military operations and "establishing more stable Governments than those [previously] established," it seems certain that he contemplated further territorial aggrandizement. In his annual message to Congress (December 1847), Polk called for annexation of New Mexico and the Californias (in the plural, thus including Baja California), and he threatened to up the ante because of "the obstinate perseverance of Mexico in protracting the war." If Mexico would not submit, Polk warned, the United States must "tak[e] the full measure of indemnity into our own hands"—that is, the United States must permanently seize even more territory. But guerrilla warfare against the American armies apparently had turned Polk against his original idea of seizing all of Mexico north of the twenty-sixth parallel: he seems now to have hoped instead to grab the Mexican port of Tampico (at the twenty-second parallel); to secure an American right of passage across the isthmus of Tehuantepec, from the Gulf of Mexico to the Pacific Ocean; and "perhaps to make the Sierra Madra [*sic*] the line," thus seizing the province of Tamaulipas and all the rest of Mexico between these mountains and the Gulf of Mexico.

The Mexicans had surprised Polk by their stubborn resistance to his idea that they should acknowledge defeat and sign a peace treaty. Consequently, the war had dragged on much longer than the president had anticipated. During this time a series of military triumphs fed American patriotic fervor, especially in the South and Southwest, from which a disproportionate number of the American soldiers had been recruited. (Yet when the final toll was counted, it turned out that 14 percent of the American soldiers had died.) The Whigs had been making big gains in the midterm congressional elections, and the next presidential election was on the horizon. Public opinion was divided: some Whigs wanted no territorial conquests at all; apparently most Americans would have been satisfied to settle for New Mexico and California, and they wanted an end to the war; but vociferous groups within the Democratic Party sought even more territory from Mexico.

Successful Negotiation, at Last

Favoring this last course, Polk aimed to increase the pressure on Mexico by recalling his envoy, Nicholas Trist, rather than amending Trist's original instructions. Thus when Trist—violating repeated orders to return home—remained in Mexico City and finally secured a treaty consonant with those original instructions, Polk had no firm ground on which to reject the work of his insubordinate emissary. Trist had even acquired California and New Mexico for only $15 million, although authorized to pay $20 million. Yet astonishingly, because on November 16, 1847, Trist had received the orders to leave Mexico, the angry president refused to pay Trist's salary for the period—November 16, 1847, through February 2, 1848—during which he had skillfully negotiated the treaty that secured everything he had previously been instructed to get. Nevertheless, and inconsistently, Polk probably breathed a sigh of relief that Trist had enabled the United States to terminate without loss of face a war in which American losses had been considerable. The president, however, would assume no responsibility himself for ending hostilities, leaving it instead to the senators— eleven of whose appetites for Mexican soil remained unsatiated— to decide for themselves whether or not to halt the war with territorial acquisitions smaller than Polk had originally desired. Trist's treaty added a mere 650,000 square miles to U.S. territory, whereas Polk had once hoped for about 950,000 square miles. Happily, the war was by now sufficiently unpopular in the United States that the Senate eventually voted by thirty-eight to fourteen (with four dissatisfied senators abstaining) to accept Trist's treaty. Part of the opposition or abstention came from senators—like slave-state Senators James Westcott, Dixon Lewis, Sam Houston, and David Atchison and the Illinois Senator Stephen Douglas (whose wife stood to inherit over 100 slaves and a great Mississippi plantation from her rich father)—who would have liked hundreds of thousands of square miles more of Mexican territory.

Polk's unsettling experiences in governing his slaves may illuminate how he conducted diplomacy and the war. Having been subjected when he was sixteen to an excruciating (unanesthetized), pioneering operation to remove a urinary stone, and having grown up a frail and relatively bookish youth (whose later marriage remained childless), Polk always felt a need to prove himself. When he compromised with his fugitive slaves (having them whipped but then sometimes selling a favored bondsman into the slave's familiar central Tennessee homeland or requiring that Dismukes's whipping of Gilbert and Addison be witnessed by Polk's agent Bobbitt), these halfway measures were ineffectual in curbing flight. Unsatisfying experiences of this sort may have reinforced Polk's feeling that he must act in an authoritative, decisive way if his presidency was to be a success. Once president, he immediately effected Texas annexation in the speediest possible manner, disregarding the outcry this aroused; he took an aggressive stance toward Britain, depending on the Senate to assume responsibility for retreating from his untenable territorial claims against Canada; he forced through Congress a hasty declaration of war on Mexico; and he pursued against Mexico territorial ambitions predictably unacceptable to any government of that nation, once again depending on the Senate to take responsibility for backing down from his most far-reaching goals. These seem to be the actions of a man who felt he must prove himself, not only by being a workaholic, but also by repeatedly flexing his muscle in order to achieve his foreign policy goals. May not the humiliations Polk had experienced in governing his slaves have contributed to his determination to show the Mexicans, and even the powerful British, who was boss?

American expansion to the Pacific has often seemed predetermined, as Manifest Destiny, but it need not have been precisely so. Had Henry Clay been elected in 1844, he would not have demanded the Rio Grande as Texas's border, and this rich source for dispute with Mexico would not have existed. Mexico, then, might well have accepted—at least informally, if not soon by formal agreement—the annexation of Texas to the United States, especially if financial compensation had been tendered. American settlers (mostly from the North) would then have infiltrated California, as Americans (mostly from the South) had previously done in Texas; and quickly a movement for Californian autonomy, followed by independence from Mexico, would have ensued, similar to the one that had already succeeded in Texas. California no doubt would then have been annexed to the United States. This whole process would have been accelerated by the Gold Rush (which of course no one could foresee). Mexico probably would have tried to put a military halt to the process, but its efforts would probably have been even less effectual than they had been against Texas. No protracted war—perhaps no war at all—had to have occurred. The boundary between the United States and Mexico would *not* be identical to the present boundary: Texas would not extend southward quite as far as the Rio Grande, and the Mexican border might extend many miles into present-day New Mexico. Would this diminution of U.S. territory have been worthwhile for the sake of avoiding an aggressive and unjust war against Mexico? In particular, would it have been worthwhile if—by renouncing an extended war against Mexico—the Americans had been able to avoid the bloodbath that followed so soon thereafter, the American Civil War?

Mexican Landowners Were Treated Unfairly

by *Hutchings' California Magazine*

From May 13, 1846, to May 30, 1848, the United States and Mexico were at war over territorial disputes. The U.S. victory in the Mexican War greatly increased the size of the United States: The provisions of the Treaty of Guadalupe Hidalgo, ratified on May 30, 1848, included the cession of 55 percent of Mexico's territory, an area comprising present-day Arizona, California, New Mexico, Texas, and parts of Colorado, Nevada, and Utah. Mexico received $15 million in exchange. The treaty also set the Texas border at the Rio Grande River and provided for the protection of the property and civil rights of Mexican nationals living within the new border.

These acquisitions satisfied those who sought to extend the United States to the Pacific Coast, but the additional territory eventually proved problematic in the slave state–free state debates of the 1850s. It also posed a series of legal problems concerning land ownership for Mexican nationals living in the territories ceded to the United States.

California was an especially contentious area. The 1848 discovery of gold at Sutter's Mill sparked a gold rush and a sudden population increase leading to clashes over land between established Mexicans and American newcomers. The following article, from *Hutchings' California Magazine* of July 1857, describes the problems encountered by landowning Mexicans after the American

---

Hutchings' California Magazine, "Land Loss in California," July 1857.

takeover of California. The new American laws often contradicted
existing Mexican statutes, resulting in a great deal of confusion and
hardship for the landowners. The article criticizes the way the U.S.
government handled the territorial transition and treated the resident
Mexicans ("Californios").

The establishment of the American dominion in California,
made it necessary that the titles to land, owned in the State,
under grants from Mexico, should be recognized and protected in accordance with the principles of American law. Protection was due to the land owners under the general principles of equity and the laws of nations, and had been expressly provided in
the treaty of Guadalupe Hidalgo. It was necessary that the protection should be in accordance with the principles of American
law, because the vast majority of the population soon came to be
composed of Americans, who naturally introduced their own system of law,—the only system suited to their method of conduct-
ing business.

The Mexican System and American Laws

But there was a question of much difficulty as to how this protection should be furnished. The Mexican titles were lacking in many
of the conditions necessary to a perfect title under the American
laws. The land systems of the two countries were constructed on
entirely different principles and with different objects. The Mexican system was a good one for the purposes to be attained by it; it
was suited to the wants of the natives of California. They were
stockgrowers;—their only occupation, and wealth and staple food
was furnished by their herds. They owned immense numbers of
horses and horned cattle, and to furnish them with pasture, each
ranchero required a large tract of land, which might be used by his
own stock, exclusively. The public land in California was very extensive; it was worth nothing; there was little demand for it; no
evils had been experienced, none were feared from the accumulation of great tracts, in the hands of a few owners; every grant was
supposed to be a benefit to the State, by furnishing a home to a new
citizen; and so, large grants were made without stint, on nearly
every application. If the applicant could show that the land was
public property, and unoccupied, he could obtain from 10,000 to
50,000 acres without expense, on condition that he would make the

ranch his home, build a house on it, and place several hundred head of horned cattle upon it. These grants were usually made without any accurate description of the land; there never had been any government survey of any portion of the territory; there were no surveyors in the country to locate the boundaries; neither would the applicants have been willing in most cases to pay for surveys; nor was there any apparent need for them, land being very cheap and quarrels about boundaries very rare. Sometimes the land granted was described with certain fixed natural boundaries. In other cases, the grant might be described as lying in a narrow valley, between two ranges of mountains, and extending from a tree, rock, or clump of willows, up or down the valley far enough to include three, six, or ten square leagues. The most common form of grant was for a certain number of square leagues, lying in a much larger district, bounded by well known land-marks. Thus the famous Mariposa grant of Fremont is for ten square leagues 11,386 acres, equivalent to a tract about nine miles square—in the district bounded by the San Joaquin river on the west, the Sierra Nevada mountains on the east, the Merced river on the north, and the Chowchillas on the south; which district includes nearly 100 square leagues. Under such a grant, the Mexican law allowed the grantee to select any place, within the larger limits, and make it his home.

The grants made were not carefully registered. The law prescribed that the petitions for land should all be preserved, and a record of them kept, and that a registry should be made of all the lands granted; but the affairs of the Governor's office were loosely conducted; and in many cases where the claimants have been in possession for twenty years, and have an undoubted title, there is nothing in the archives or records of the former government to show for it. In many respects the California governor had been very careless about granting lands. Some times they would grant the same lands to several persons; and there was one instance wherein Gov. Micheltorena ordered that every person in the northern District of California, who had petitioned for land before a certain date, and whose petition had not been acted upon, should be the owner of the land asked for; provided the nearest Alcalde should certify that it belonged to the public domain. In these cases no title to the grantees was ever made by the Governor.

I have thus briefly mentioned the main peculiarities of the Mexican system of disposing of the public land in California, as distinguished from the American system. The Mexican government made no survey of the land; granted it away in immense tracts without any fixed boundaries, leaving the grantee a wide discretion in regard to location, and keeping no careful registry of the grants.

Lose Land or Sue the Government

When the great immigration of '49 filled the land with Americans, it became necessary to provide for the recognition and protection of the good Mexican titles by the American Courts. But how was this to be done? By the ordinary State Courts? The judges would not be sufficiently able, and would be ignorant of the laws under which the grants had been made; and the juries would be composed of Americans whose interests would lead them to do injustice to the large land-owners. Besides, the lawmakers and judges elected by a deeply interested populace could not be depended upon to do justice under such circumstances.

Or should the protection be rendered by the appointment of a commission, instructed to make a summary examination of all claims, declare all those valid which had been in possession previous to the conquest, and of which some record might be found in the archives; leaving the other claims to be tried in the U.S. Courts? This was the policy which should have been pursued.

But that plan was not to prevail. . . . [The] bill "to ascertain and settle the private land claims in the State of California". . .provides for the appointment of a special Judicial Committee (to be composed of three judges), before which all claimants to land, in the State, under Mexican titles, should bring suit against the Federal Government within two years after the date of the act, under penalty of forfeiting their land. It provided further, that a law agent should be appointed, who should "superintend the interests of the United States in every case." It provided further, that appeals might be taken in these land cases, from the judgments of the Commission to the U.S. District Court, and from the latter, to the Supreme Court of the United States. It provided further, that in the trial of these cases, the Commission and the courts should "be governed by the treaty of Guadalupe Hidalgo, the law of nations, the laws, usages and customs of the country from which the claim is derived, the principles of equity, and the decisions of the Supreme Court of the United States."

This act provided that the owners of land should sue the Government or lose their land. But why be subjected to so severe a condition? The land owners had committed no offence, that they should be threatened with spoliation. It was not their fault that the Mexican land system differed from the American. The introduction of a new system by the Government did not justify the invalidation of titles, which had been good before, and the subjection of the owners to tedious and expensive litigation. When the American Government took California, it was in honor bound to leave the titles to property as secure as they were at the time of the transfer, and express provision to this effect was made in the treaty. Let us imagine that California were to be again transferred to some other power, whose land system is far more complex and strict than our own, and that all our present titles should be declared incomplete and insecure, and that every land owner should be taxed to one-fourth of the value of his land to pay for defending his title before a foreign and hostile Court, and, if successful, should not get his title until six or eight years after the commencement of the litigation;—would we not exclaim against it as extremely unjust? But what is the difference between that supposed case and the actual one under consideration? There is no difference between the principles involved in the two cases; each supposes a great wrong—such a wrong as has been committed by the Federal Government of the United States upon holders of land in California under Mexican grants.

812 Landowners File Suit

The Land Commission was opened in this city, January 1st, 1852, and in the ensuing fourteen months, 812 suits were brought, and these were all decided previous to the 3d of March, 1855, at which time the Commission dissolved.

It was severe hardship for owners of land under grants from Mexico, that they should be required to sue the government of the United States (which ought to have protected—not persecuted them) or lose their land; but this hardship was rendered much more severe by the peculiar circumstances under which the suits had to be tried. The trials were to be had in San Francisco at a time when the expenses of traveling and of living in San Francisco were very great, and the fees of lawyers enormous. The prosecution of the suits required a study of the laws of Mexico, in regard to the disposition of the public lands, and this study had, of course, to be paid for by the clients. In many cases the claimants had to come to San Francisco from remote parts of the State; having three hundred miles to travel, bringing their witnesses with them at their own expense. The witnesses were nearly all native Californians, and it was necessary to employ interpreters at high prices.

Meanwhile the claimant could not dispose of his land, on account of the cloud there was on his title: neither could he have it surveyed by the U.S. Surveyor so as to give notice to the public where his land really lay. As he could not give a secure title, nor, in most cases, tell where his boundaries were, the Americans were not disposed to buy the land. Many squatters were, no doubt, glad of a pretext under which they might take other people's land and use it without paying rent; but the circumstances were often such that they were justified in refusing to buy. The number of settlers or squatters became large; they formed a decided majority of the voters in several of the counties; their political influence was great; politicians bowed down before them; all political parties courted them; and most of the U.S. Land Agents, and District Attorneys, appointed under the influence of the California Congressmen, became the representatives of the settler interest, and failed to represent the true interest of the United States. Every device known to the law was resorted to defeat the claimant, or delay the confirmation of his grant, as though it were the interest of the Federal Government to defeat every claimant, or to postpone his success as long as possible.

Eight hundred and twelve important suits, to be tried according to the principles of strange laws, and on evidence given in a strange tongue, and where the testimony, in many of the cases, covered hundreds of pages of manuscript, were not to be disposed of in any brief period. In fact, the Commission did not clear its docket until more than three years after its organization. This delay, which would have been disastrous in any country, was doubly so in California. During the greater portion of this time, the titles to most of the good farming land in the settled districts of the State, were declared to be unsettled. The delay was an encouragement to dishonest, and often a justification of honest squatters. They wanted to cultivate the ground; they could not learn whether the land they wished to occupy was public or private property; they knew the question would not be decided soon, and therefore they might know, if dishonest, that they might make a profit by seizing land which they were morally certain would be, and should be, confirmed to the claimant; and if honest, they could not be expected to pay for property, to which, in many cases, the title was one in which they could place no confidence. The consequence of the system was, that a large portion of the most valuable farming land in the State was occupied by squatters. This occupation contributed greatly to injure the value of the property. The land owner could not sell his land, nor use it, and yet he was compelled to pay taxes. His ranch brought serious evils upon him. It was the seat of a multitude of squatters, who—as a necessary consequence of antagonistic pecuniary interest,—were his bitter enemies. Cases we know, where they fenced in his best land; laid their claims between his house and his garden; threatened to shoot him if he should trespass on their inclosure; killed his cattle if they broke through the sham fences; cut down his valuable shade and fruit trees, and sold them for fire-wood; made no permanent improvements, and acted generally as tho' they were determined to make all the immediate profit possible, out of the ranch. Such things were not rare: they are familiar to every person who knows the general course of events during the last five years in Sonoma, Solano, Contra Costa, Santa Clara, Santa Cruz and Monterey Counties. Blood was not unfrequently spilled in consequence of the feuds between the land holders and the squatters; the victims in nearly every case, belonging to the former class.

After the Federal Government had committed the error of compelling every Californian land owner to bring suit for his own land, which he had held in indisputable ownership under the Mexican dominion, and even before the independence of Mexico and Spain, and after the Government stubbornly contested every case before a tribunal whose learning, ability, and honesty, was and is, universally admitted,—after all this, it is strange that those persons, whose claims were confirmed, and who had been in possession of their land before the American conquest, and in cases where there was no suspicion of fraud, were not allowed to take their own property once for all. But no; Uncle Sam told all the Californians who had gained their suits, that they should not take their land till they had sued him again; he would appeal every case; the claimant must make another fight for his property, or be despoiled.

An Injurious Policy

Here then, was the whole work to be gone over again in the Federal District Courts, of which there are two in the State; and in each district there are about four hundred claims, to be tried by a judge, much of whose time is occupied with the trial of admiralty cases. The land suits must all be defended, or attended to, by the

United States District Attorney, much of whose time is occupied with criminal cases, and civil business in which the Federal Government is interested. The result is delay upon delay. . . .

Only two pleas have been made to extenuate or justify the stubborn opposition made by the agents of the Government to the recognition of the Californian land holders. These pleas are, first, that many of the claims are fraudulent; and, secondly, that the Californians claim too much land.

It is not true that many of the claims are fraudulent. The Land Commission did not reject one claim, and the District Courts have rejected only two, on the ground of fraud. There may be twenty-five fraudulent claims in all; I believe not more. There may be many claims which would not have been valid under the Mexican law; but these are not fraudulent, and have been, or will be rejected. But even if there were a hundred, that would be no reason why the Government should attempt to rob the holders of land under titles undoubtedly good in equity and under the Mexican law. A distinction might be made between the two classes, of the suspicious and the undoubtedly good claims. But the Federal Government made no distinction. The Peralta grant, which was made in the last century, and has been in constant possession ever since, under a perfect title according to the Mexican law, was subjected to the same litigation and vexatious delay, and was given over to the tender mercies of the squatters in the same manner with the most questionable title in all the land.

The other plea is still worse. It may be that the welfare of the people requires the land to be equally divided among them; but shall that justify the Government in robbing—directly by violence, or indirectly by litigation—the owners of large tracts? If it be wrong for me to rob my neighbor of his dollars, is it right for Uncle Sam to rob Peralta, or any other Californian, of his land? And let it be remembered that temporary dispossession is morally as wrong as entire and final spoliation. I admit that it were far better for the country that the Mexican grant-holders should not own so much land; I admit that it were better, looking at the question abstractly, that the settlers should own all the land they claim, I admit that the settlers are more active and industrious, and contribute vastly more, in proportion to their means, to the development and wealth of the State, than do the native holders of the large grants; but all this has nothing to do with the main question. . . .

Not only has the system adopted by the Federal Government,

in regard to Mexican grants, been most injurious and unjust to the claimants, but it has also been very injurious to the country at large. It has deprived the people in the most populous agricultural districts, of permanent titles; has prevented the erection of fine houses, valuable improvements, permanent homes; has contributed to make the population unsettled; to keep families from coming to the country; and, in fine, has been one of the chief causes of the present unsound condition of the social and business relations of California.

8 The First U.S. Woman's Rights Convention
Convenes: July 19–20, 1848

Courage and Vision Launched the Women's Movement

by Eleanor Flexner

On July 19 and 20, 1848, the first American woman's rights convention assembled at the Wesleyan Methodist Church in Seneca Falls, New York. The meeting in Seneca Falls marks the beginning of the organized women's movement. The leaders of the convention, Lucretia Mott and Elizabeth Cady Stanton, decided to focus their attention on woman's rights after they and other women were denied seats at the World Anti-Slavery Conference in London in 1840.

Both Mott and Stanton, frustrated by this slight, resolved to address bias against women upon their return to the United States. At that time in America, women were not allowed to vote, hold office, or sit on juries. Married women were legally subservient to their husbands; for example, wives could not hold assets or keep earned income in their own name.

After several years of establishing contacts and exchanging ideas, Mott, Stanton, and other woman's rights reformers planned a convention. On July 14, 1848, the women issued the Declaration of Sentiments, a proclamation that expressed their objectives using the Declaration of Independence as a model. When the convention assembled a few days later, more than three hundred people attended (about forty of whom were men). Eleven resolutions, in-

Eleanor Flexner, *Century of Struggle: The Woman's Rights Movement in the United States.* Cambridge, MA: The Belknap Press of Harvard University Press, 1959. Copyright © 1959 by Eleanor Flexner. Reproduced by permission of the publisher.

cluding one calling for universal women's suffrage, were adopted at the convention.

The following selection by Eleanor Flexner traces the Seneca Falls Convention from its roots in 1840 through its culmination in July 1848. Flexner examines the roles of Lucretia Mott and Elizabeth Cady Stanton. She also discusses the drafting of the Declaration of Sentiments and the place of the Seneca Falls Convention in the history of the woman's rights movement.

Woman's rights activist Eleanor Flexner is the author of *Century of Struggle: The Woman's Rights Movement in the United States*, a groundbreaking work in women's studies that has been published in several languages.

Grievances, even articulate voices raised in discontent, are not enough to give birth to a reform movement. What was needed now was a sharp impetus—leadership and; above all, a program. These were to be the achievement of the Seneca Falls convention in the summer of 1848, from which the inception of the woman's rights movement in the United States is commonly dated.

The Seeds of the Convention Idea

Although it grew naturally out of the unsatisfactory position of women in a changing world and the work of the pioneers during the preceding thirty years, the seed of the convention was actually planted in the summer of 1840. A World Anti-Slavery Convention in London was attended by an American delegation which included a number of women; but despite the strong objections of some of the American leaders, the convention ruled, after hot debate, that only men delegates should be seated. Among the women compelled to sit passively in the galleries during the ensuing ten days were Lucretia Mott and the young wife of an abolitionist leader, Elizabeth Cady Stanton.

After the sessions the two women walked the London streets together or sat on a bench in the British Museum while the rest of their party explored its treasures, talking about the anomaly of devoted workers in the anti-slavery cause being denied any voice in its deliberations simply because they were women, and the need for action.

In these talks Mrs. Mott was the preceptor; aided by the cir-

cumstances of birth and religious faith, she had already cast off
many of the bonds that trammeled other women. . . .

The Role of Elizabeth Cady Stanton

In an age that abounded in stormy personalities that clashed continually even if they had common aims, Mrs. Mott was widely
beloved. A gentle manner, luminous countenance, and soft voice
concealed an inflexible rectitude and devotion to principle. In some
respects initially conservative (she drew back at first from demands
she felt too precipitate, such as the franchise and easier divorce
laws), she never shrank from the conclusions which a fearless and
rational mind imposed on her. Her contribution in helping to free
the gifted and eager mind of Elizabeth Cady Stanton was an incal-
culable one, for the younger woman was destined to be the leading intellectual force in the emancipation of American women. . . .

In 1840 she married Henry B. Stanton, an abolitionist leader
who had faced down angry mobs. She also made friends with the
Grimké sisters. After her meeting with Lucretia Mott in London
the friendship was maintained by correspondence when the Stan-
tons moved to Boston, where they made their first home. When
Mrs. Stanton visited in Johnstown, she got in a little work with Al-
bany legislators on behalf of the Married Woman's Property Bill
which finally became New York state law early in 1848. But the
decisive turn in her life came when the family moved to Seneca
Falls, in the Finger Lakes region of New York, and Elizabeth Cady
Stanton suddenly came face to face with the realities of a house-
wife's drudgery and isolation in a small town. Her husband was
often away on business, and she was left with a growing family of
lively children, most of them boys who got into constant mischief.
There was the usual servant problem, and even when she could
get help, like all other housewives of her day, she did an immense
amount of work: baking and cooking, washing and sewing, and
caring for each new baby. With her restless and eager mind she
found the situation, despite all the reading she managed to squeeze
in, an intolerable one:

> I now fully understood the practical difficulties most women had
> to contend with in the isolated household, and the impossibility of
> woman's best development if in contact, the chief part of her life,
> with servants and children. . . . Emerson says: "A healthy discon-
> tent is the first step to progress." The general discontent I felt with

woman's portion as wife, mother, housekeeper, physician, and spiritual guide, the chaotic condition into which everything fell without her constant supervision, and the wearied, anxious look of the majority of women, impressed me with the strong feeling that some active measures should be taken to remedy the wrongs of society in general and of women in particular. My experiences at the World Anti-Slavery Convention, all I had read of the legal status of women, and the oppression I saw everywhere, together swept across my soul, intensified now by many personal experiences. It seemed as if all the elements had conspired to impel me to some onward step. I could not see what to do or where to begin—my only thought was a public meeting for protest and discussion.

Deciding to Call a Convention

The possibility of such a meeting had been discussed by Mrs. Stanton and Mrs. Mott from their first acquaintance. But no opportunity to realize it occurred until the Motts paid a visit in Waterloo, New York, near Seneca Falls, where Mrs. Stanton spent a day with them. There she also found the Motts' hostess Jane Hunt, Martha Wright (Mrs. Mott's sister), and Mary Ann McClintock, all of them Quakers. To them "I poured out, that day, the torrent of my long accumulating discontent, with such vehemence and indignation that I stirred myself, as well as the rest of the party, to do and dare anything."

Seated around a mahogany table (now in the Smithsonian Institution in Washington), the five women decided to call a convention (today we would simply call it a meeting since there were to be no elected delegates), and wrote an announcement which appeared in the next day's issue (July 14) of the *Seneca County Courier:*

> Woman's Rights Convention—A convention to discuss the social, civil and religious rights of woman will be held in the Wesleyan Chapel, Seneca Falls, New York, on Wednesday and Thursday, the 19th and 20th of July current; commencing at 10 a.m. During the first day the meeting will be held exclusively for women, who are earnestly invited to attend. The public generally are invited to be present on the second day, when Lucretia Mott of Philadelphia and other ladies and gentlemen will address the convention.

Having drafted the notice, the women were at a loss as to how to proceed. Obviously what was required was some kind of declaration of sentiments, such as they were familiar with from their experiences with anti-slavery gatherings. But what form it should take, they had no idea. When Mrs. Stanton began to read aloud from the Declaration of Independence, it seemed to lend itself to their purpose; the resulting paraphrase of the original, sentence by sentence and paragraph by paragraph, became a Declaration of Principles that would serve three generations of women:

> When, in the course of human events, it becomes necessary for one portion of the family of man to assume among the people of the earth a position different from that they have hitherto occupied. . . .

> We hold these truths to be self-evident: that all men and women are created equal; that they are endowed by their Creator with certain inalienable rights: that among these are life, liberty and the pursuit of happiness. . . .

> The history of mankind is a history of repeated injuries and usurpations on the part of man toward woman, having in direct object the establishment of an absolute tyranny over her. To prove this, let facts be submitted to a candid world.

The facts presented ranged over every aspect of woman's status. In conclusion, departing from its model, the Declaration stated:

> In entering upon the great work before us, we anticipate no small amount of misconception, misrepresentation, and ridicule; but we shall use every instrumentality within our power to effect our object. We shall employ agents, circulate tracts, petition the State and national legislatures, and endeavor to enlist the pulpit and the press on our behalf. We hope this Convention will be followed by a series of Conventions embracing every part of the country.

The final drafting of resolutions to implement the Declaration was turned over to Mrs. Stanton, and the Motts went home to Philadelphia, leaving the young woman to cope with her household, and with a rising sense of panic. The latter was in no way mitigated when she read her husband the draft of a resolution she proposed demanding the vote for women; Henry B. Stanton declared that if it were presented to the convention he would have nothing to do with the affair, and that he would leave town. (He did.) To make matters worse, a letter arrived from Mrs. Mott, mixing encouragement with caution:

I requested (Mary Ann McClintock) . . . to tell thee how poorly my husband was, and that it is not likely that I should be able to go to Seneca Falls before the morning of the convention. I hope however that he will be able to be present the second day. . . . James says thy *great* speech thou must reserve for the second day, so that he and others may be able to hear it. The convention will not be as large as it otherwise might be, owing to the busy time with the farmers, harvest, etc. But it will be a beginning, and we hope it will be followed in due time by one of a more general character.

None of the women, even Lucretia Mott, felt equal to the task of serving as chairman, and it had been planned that James Mott would fill the post. Fortunately he recovered promptly and both the Motts arrived in Seneca Falls in good time. Less auspicious was Mrs. Mott's reaction to the proposed resolution on the franchise: "Thou will make us ridiculous. We must go slowly." Only Frederick Douglass, the Negro abolitionist leader who published his paper, *The North Star*, in near-by Rochester, approved of Mrs. Stanton's daring proposal; reassured by his promise that he would be present and take the floor in her support, she resolved to stick to her purpose.

Launching a Movement

July 19, 1848, was a fine summer morning, and despite the demands of the haying season, and the fact that only one issue of the *Seneca Courier* had carried the brief notice, Mrs. Mott's fears were not realized. People came from a radius of fifty miles to the little Wesleyan chapel, which the convention initiators found locked when they arrived. (Perhaps a reluctant minister had regretted his rash act in making his premises available for such an occasion.) But the delay was brief; a nephew of Mrs. Stanton's was boosted through a window and the gathering crowd flocked inside.

One of the women told, some sixty years later, of the impression the proceedings made on a farmer's daughter. Nineteen-year-old Charlotte Woodward, who longed to be a typesetter and work in a print shop, and who might as well have aspired to fly to the moon, read the *Courier* notice and ran from one neighbor to another, to find that others had already read it, some with amused incredulity, others with the same excitement as herself. She and half a dozen of her friends planned to attend the convention, and set off early in the morning of the 19th in a wagon drawn by farm horses, fearful that they would be the only ladies present. But as they neared Seneca Falls they met many other vehicles like theirs, headed for the same destination. She sat for two days, late into the evening, in a back row, among an audience of some three hundred; no less than forty men had turned up the first day, originally planned for ladies only, and had compelled the women to modify this restriction. She heard Elizabeth Cady Stanton rise to make her maiden speech:

> I should feel exceedingly diffident to appear before you at this time, having never before spoken in public, were I not nerved by a sense of right and duty, did I not feel that the time had come for the question of woman's wrongs to be laid before the public, did I not believe that woman herself must do this work; for woman alone can understand the height, the depth, the length and the breadth of her degradation.

There followed a speech almost incredible for a novice: long, scholarly but eloquent, of the kind that was to become familiar to Mrs. Stanton's audiences over the next fifty years. There were other speakers, and plenty of lively discussion, particularly over resolution nine, read by Mrs. Stanton: "Resolved, that it is the sacred duty of the women of this country to secure to themselves their sacred right to the elective franchise." This was the only resolution not passed unanimously; it carried by a small margin. At the conclusion of the proceedings, sixty-eight women and thirty-two men (a third of those present), signed their names to the Declaration of Principles. Among them was Charlotte Woodward who, alone of those present, lived to vote for President of the United States in 1920. [This was the first presidential election in which women were allowed to vote.]

In regarding the Seneca Falls convention as the birth of the movement for woman's rights, we are on solid ground only if we remember that birth is a stage in the whole process of growth. In this case the process had begun almost half a century earlier. Such a view does not detract from the convention's importance, or from the vision and courage of those who brought it about. They themselves were fully aware of the nature of the step they were taking; today's debt to them has been inadequately acknowledged. The Wesleyan chapel which saw their momentous gathering is marked only by a signpost on the sidewalk, and itself does service as a gas-filling station and garage.

Beginning in 1848 it was possible for women who rebelled against the circumstances of their lives, to know that they were not alone—although often the news reached them only through a vitriolic sermon or an abusive newspaper editorial. But a movement had been launched which they could either join, or ignore, that would leave its imprint on the lives of their daughters and of women throughout the world.

8

The First U.S. Woman's Rights Convention Convenes: July 19–20, 1848

The Rights of Women Must Be Acknowledged

by Elizabeth Cady Stanton

The 1840s and 1850s were decades of reform in the United States. Reformers took up a variety of social causes, from the abolition of slavery to the rights of workers. Those who sought social reform turned to the government for support and pointed out that the Constitution promoted general welfare.

Woman's rights activists, including Lucretia Mott and Elizabeth Cady Stanton, coordinated a convention in Seneca Falls, New York, on July 19 and 20, 1848, to promote their reform agenda, which centered on woman's rights. Several days before the convention, the women issued their "Declaration of Sentiments" in the *Seneca County Courier.* The document, modeled after the Declaration of Independence and written by Stanton, demanded acknowledgement of and respect for the rights of women. Sixty-eight women and thirty-two men signed the declaration, which lists eighteen grievances and emphasizes the equality of men and women.

W hen, in the course of human events, it becomes necessary for one portion of the family of man to assume among the people of the earth a position different from that which they have hitherto occupied, but one to which the laws of nature and of nature's God entitle them, a decent respect to the

---

Elizabeth Cady Stanton, *The Declaration of Sentiments*. Seneca Falls Conference, Seneca Falls, New York, 1848.

opinions of mankind requires that they should declare the causes that impel them to such a course.

The Patient Sufferance of Women

We hold these truths to be self-evident: that all men and women are created equal; that they are endowed by their Creator with certain inalienable rights; that among these are life, liberty, and the pursuit of happiness; that to secure these rights governments are instituted, deriving their just powers from the consent of the governed. Whenever any form of government becomes destructive of these ends, it is the right of those who suffer from it to refuse allegiance to it, and to insist upon the institution of a new government, laying its foundation on such principles, and organizing its powers in such form, as to them shall seem most likely to effect their safety and happiness. Prudence, indeed, will dictate that governments long established should not be changed for light and transient causes; and accordingly all experience hath shown that mankind are more disposed to suffer, while evils are sufferable, than to right themselves by abolishing the forms to which they are accustomed. But when a long train of abuses and usurpations, pursuing invariably the same object, evinces a design to reduce them under absolute despotism, it is their duty to throw off such government, and to provide new guards for their future security. Such has been the patient sufferance of the women under this government, and such is now the necessity which constrains them to demand the equal station to which they are entitled. The history of mankind is a history of repeated injuries and usurpations on the part of man toward woman, having in direct object the establishment of an absolute tyranny over her. To prove this, let facts be submitted to a candid world.

He has never permitted her to exercise her inalienable right to the elective franchise.

He has compelled her to submit to laws, in the formation of which she had no voice.

He has withheld from her rights which are given to the most ignorant and degraded men—both natives and foreigners. . . .

He has made her, if married, in the eye of the law, civilly dead.

He has taken from her all right in property, even to the wages she earns.

He has made her, morally, an irresponsible being, as she can commit many crimes with impunity, provided they be done in the presence of her husband. In the covenant of marriage, she is compelled to promise obedience to her husband, he becoming, to all intents and purposes, her master—the law giving him power to deprive her of her liberty, and to administer chastisement.

He has so framed the laws of divorce, as to what shall be the proper causes, and in case of separation, to whom the guardianship of the children shall be given, as to be wholly regardles of the happiness of women—the law, in all cases, going upon a false supposition of the supremacy of man, and giving all power into his hands.

After depriving her of all rights as a married woman, if single, and the owner of property, he has taxed her to support a government which recognizes her only when her property can be made profitable to it.

He has monopolized nearly all the profitable employments, and from those she is permitted to follow, she receives but a scanty remuneration. He closes against her all the avenues to wealth and distinction which he considers most honorable to himself. As a teacher of theoloy, medicine, or law, she is not known.

He has denied her the facilities for obtaining a thorough education, all colleges being closed against her.

He allows her in church, as well as state, but a subordinate position, claiming apostolic authority for her exclusion from the ministry, and, with some exceptions, from any public participation in the affairs of the church.

He has created a false public sentiment by giving to the world a different code of morals for men and women, by which moral delinquencies which exclude women from society, are not only tolerated, but deemed of little account in man.

He has usurped the prerogative of Jehovah himself, claiming it as his right to assign for her a sphere of action, when that belongs to her conscience and to her God.

He has endeavored, in every way that he could, to destroy her confidence in her own powers, to lessen her self-respect, and to make her willing to lead a dependent and abject life.

Now, in view of this entire disfranchisement of one-half the people of this country, their social and religious degradation—in view of the unjust laws above mentioned, and because women do feel themselves aggrieved, oppressed, and fraudulently deprived of their most sacred rights, we insist that they have immediate admission to all the rights and privileges which belong to them as citizens of the United States.

The Great Exhibition of London:
May 1–October 15, 1851

The Exhibition of "Things" Influenced Culture and Advertising

by Thomas Richards

From May 1 to October 15, 1851, an event billed as "The Great Exhibition of the Industry of All Nations" was featured in Hyde Park, London. The so-called Great Exhibition was designed to display, first and foremost, products representative of Great Britain's industrial greatness. Though thirty-two other nations accepted the invitation to present "things," almost half of the fourteen thousand exhibitors were British. This collection of manufactured items, the largest ever displayed under a single roof, was housed in an impressive glass structure called the Crystal Palace. Six million visitors poured through the Crystal Palace during the five months and fifteen days of the exhibition, which was by all accounts a sensational success.

In this selection, Thomas Richards describes the Great Exhibition of 1851 as the first world's fair, department store, and shopping mall. He considers the gathering of nations to be, possibly, the most influential representative body to congregate in the nineteenth century. It fostered a spirit of competition while instilling national pride in the range of manufactures. In addition, this presentation of commodities at the Great Exhibition became a spectacle and a cultural focal point.

Thomas Richards, *The Commodity Culture of Victorian England: Advertising and Spectacle, 1851–1914*. Stanford, CA: Stanford University Press, 1990. Copyright © 1990 by the Board of Trustees of the Leland Stanford Junior University. Reproduced by permission of Stanford University Press, www.sup.org.

Richards also points out the tremendous impact the 1851 Exhibition had on advertising. Creating associations between material objects and luxury or necessity was a boon to the advertising industry. In conclusion, the author notes that the Great Exhibition of 1851 is important both for helping to establish a commodity culture—which means that manufactured goods and their display had cultural significance—and for its transformation of advertising.

I n 1851 a league of nations gathered for a congress in Hyde Park, London. Billed as a peace conference, this congress brought together the representatives of thirty-two nations from Europe, America, Africa, and the Far East. The delegations were housed in a single structure built expressly for them. The building occupied fourteen acres on the north edge of the park, and it contained, not an army of diplomats and attachés, but an assembly of manufactured articles, the largest display of commodities that had ever been brought together under one roof. The United States sent McCormick's reaper and prodigious quantities of ore; the French sent sculpture and artificial arms, hands, feet, legs, eyes; the Germans sent musical instruments and stuffed frogs; the British contributed machines. These things—tens of thousands of them packed into fourteen thousand booths—were the featured attraction at what was called "The Great Exhibition of the Industry of All Nations."

Commodities on Display

As vast as it was in execution, the Great Exhibition of 1851 had at its root a single conception: that all human life and cultural endeavor could be fully represented by exhibiting manufactured articles. As a kind of surrogate Parliament, it was perhaps the most influential representative body of the nineteenth century. For not only did it erect a monument to the commodity that lasted eighty-five years, but it also prescribed the rituals by which consumers venerated the commodity for the rest of the century. It was the first world's fair, the first department store, the first shopping mall. The Exhibition rooted the commodity in the sense of being near to the heart of things, of being caught up in the progress of people and institutions that dominated Victorian society. Until the Exhibition the commodity had not for a moment occupied center stage in English public life; during and after the Exhibition the commodity became and remained the still center of the turning earth, the focal point of all gazing and the end point of all pilgrimages. The Great Exhibition of 1851 was the first outburst of the phantasmagoria of commodity culture. It inaugurated a way of seeing things that marked indelibly the cultural and commercial life of Victorian England and fashioned a mythology of consumerism that has endured to this day.

First and foremost, this new way of seeing things was the product of a new kind of place in which things could be seen. After a long competition, the organizers of the Exhibition chose a design by Joseph Paxton, who had made a name for himself as a botanist and architect of greenhouses for the very rich. Paxton submitted a plan that called for a terraced pyramid of successively receding stories of glass and iron. The editors of *Punch* dubbed his three-tiered ziggurat the "Crystal Palace." The name stuck, and with good reason. Though the building was not crystal but plain glass, and though today it looks to us more like an overgrown greenhouse than a palace, it successfully embodied the contradictory desires and aspirations which people in the nineteenth century came more and more to attribute to manufactured things. At one and the same time the Crystal Palace was a museum and a market: it brought together a host of rare and exclusive things and promised, in a way that is very hard to pin down, that each and every one of them would one day be democratically available to anyone and everyone. The organizers of the Exhibition did not come right out and say how this would come about; rather it was the space of exhibition itself which seemed to assert that, like the feeding of the four thousand, an economic miracle was in the making. Under a single ceiling, surrounded by trees and flooded with light, commodities appeared to have come out of nowhere, radiant and ordered into departments that fixed the place of each article and gave it a caption and a numbered place in the catalogue. The Victorians never tired of admiring what the Great Exhibition did to the things they had produced; things had been exhibited before, but in 1851 the exhibited commodity became, for the first time in history, the focal point of a commodity culture.

Exhibition and Advertising

The exhibition of things had always been what the advertising industry thought it did best, but it had been exhibitionism of a limited kind on a very small scale. In Thomas Carlyle's *Past and Pre-*

sent (1843), practically all advertising takes place in the streets. Far from being carefully arranged in a clean, well-lighted space, Carlyle's advertisements are part of the unplanned and unregulated contagion of London street life. They spill out onto the streets like untreated sewage as "that great Hat seven-feet high . . . now perambulates London streets." The giant hat sponsored by a Strand hatter was only the latest addition to a crazy street scene catered to by the large and varied class of streetsellers investigated, by Henry Mayhew in *London Labour and the London Poor* (1849–54). In a few sentences Mayhew conjures up the pandemonium: "The men are standing in groups, smoking and talking; whilst the women run to and fro, some with the white round turnips showing out of their filled aprons, others with cabbages under their arms, and a piece of red-meat dangling from their hands. . . . Walnuts, blacking, apples, onions, braces, combs, turnips, herrings, pens, and corn-plaster, are all bellowed out at the same time." For all we know he might be describing a market in a painting by Brueghel rather than the scene at Brill, one of over forty open-air markets left in mid-Victorian London. As Fernand Braudel has shown, the sight, smell, and feel of goods in bulk that permeated open-air markets all over Europe changed little from the sixteenth through the early nineteenth centuries. The same can be said for the practices of early Victorian advertisers, who are, despite all their clever little gimmicks, the lineal descendants of the Pardoner with his bottle of pig's bones [the Pardoner is an untrustworthy character from the fourteenth-century *Canterbury Tales;* Autolycus of Greek mythology was a master thief] and Autolycus with his bag of tricks.

After the Great Exhibition of 1851 this traditional kind of advertising became obsolete and increasingly untenable. In an 1863 book called *Advertise: How? When? Where?* William Smith tried to explain what had happened to his business: "How to advertise? That question is very readily answered. Go to the nearest printer's; order a quantity of handbills; let a man deliver them to all the passers-by; send to the daily and weekly papers; and the thing's done. Is it? The thing *was* done thus in the good old jog-trot days of our ancestors, but we live in the nineteenth century—the age of wonders, of *Scientific Balloon Ascents, Great Exhibitions, and Underground Railways.* So far from the old proverb holding good, there is nothing under the sun that is *not* new." Smith is truly a prophet of modern advertising. In the wake of the Great Exhibition, not only does he assert that advertisers ought to exploit these new technologies so as to monopolize all attention, he is aware that these technologies have permanently altered the conditions of advertising. Spectacle has become paramount. The commodities in the Crystal Palace are no longer the trivial things that Marx had once said they could be mistaken for; they are a sensual feast for the eye of the spectator, and they have taken on the ceremonial trappings of the dominant institutions and vested interests of mid-Victorian England. In his little book, which later went through twenty-three editions, Smith was one of the first in advertising to acknowledge the power of spectacle in organizing and channeling signification around and through manufactured objects.

One particular moment of spectacle—the Great Exhibition of 1851—helped to shape the way advertisers represented commodities for the rest of the century and to define the most familiar imperatives of modern commodity culture. No single element of the Crystal Palace was new; the Victorian taste for luxury, ostentation, and outward show had long been reflected on the stage as well as on the street and inside the home. What the Crystal Palace did was to synthesize and systematize these elements of spectacle by putting them all together under one roof in the service of manufactured objects. The Great Exhibition of Things made it possible to talk expressively and excessively about commodities, and it opened up vast areas of social and institutional life that had previously been closed off to advertisers. In 1843 the *Edinburgh Review* had castigated advertisers for fabricating most of their product endorsements, and Carlyle had taken them to task for making "true proclamation if that will do; if that will not, then false proclamation." Eight years later England was flooded with true proclamations affirming the value of things. Famous men like the Prince Consort were now praising commodities; the nations of the earth chose them as their representatives; professional and scientific organizations showed their prowess and charted their progress by displaying them. Every walk of life and every part of the human body now seemed to have some kind of commodity ministering to it. The title page of the one-volume *Official Catalogue* may have insisted that "the earth is the Lord's, and all that therein is," but it would have been altogether more fitting and proper had the Exhibition taken Ecclesiastes 5:11 as its text: "Where much is, there are many to consume it; and what hath the owner but the sight of it with his eyes?". . .

A New Culture of "Things"

The Great Exhibition of 1851 represents a pivotal moment in the history of advertising, for the particular style it created for the commodity ultimately transformed the advertising industry and contributed to the formation of a new commodity culture in Victorian England. Many firms considered the Exhibition the best publicity they had ever had, and for years afterwards advertisers venerated the event without understanding exactly what it had done to their business. In *Advertising: How? When? Where?* William Smith saw clearly enough that "the Great Exhibition seemed to give an immense impetus to advertising," but he immediately qualified this by adding that "there has not been the improvement in the various modes of appealing to public notice that we might have expected." Smith goes on to complain about the flimsy paper, poor graphics, and bad grammar of most advertising in the 1860's. The advertising industry took a long time to realize that the Great Exhibition had created a new cultural form for the representation of commodities. Though at different times and under different circumstances the industry attempted to recover something of the charisma the Great Exhibition had temporarily conferred on commodities, it was not until the 1880's that commodities were again able to achieve a monopoly of signification in the public sphere. In part, the Great Exhibition had exalted commodities because it had been an event designed expressly to exalt them. But if for a short period of time the Exhibition also brought about the apotheosis of the commodity, it was because it had managed to synthesize and refine a particular cultural form for the representation of manufactured things: spectacle.

The Victorian taste for spectacle is well known and has been well documented. It consisted primarily of a rhetorical mode of amplification and excess that came to pervade and structure public and private life in the nineteenth century, and it originated in the legitimation crisis that followed in the wake of the French Revolution and the Napoleonic Wars. In the eighteenth century carefully orchestrated displays of secular and sacred power had been the prerogative of ancien-régime monarchs. In the nineteenth century, most of the rituals that fixed a king firmly at the center of a long-standing hierarchical order had disappeared even in England, where the monarchy remained embodied in the moribund figures of George III and George IV. But the need for legitimating the new bourgeois order remained, and the class that came to dominate the nineteenth century found it was better to update the old forms of spectacle than do away with them altogether or invent new ones. Since most societies, even societies undergoing revolutions, find it much easier to assert some kind of continuity with the past rather than to break cleanly from it, most forms of legitimation, even the ones employed by revolutionary leaders like Lenin and Mao [in the twentieth century, Lenin was a revolutionary leader in Russia, and Mao led a Chinese revolution] must at the very least conjure up the shade of the past in order to banish it forever into oblivion. Even in the extreme examples contained in books like [Aldous Huxley's] *Brave New World* and [George Orwell's] *1984* where old ways have continued outside the pale of new social orders, societies do not succeed in manufacturing a total break with the past, thus putting totally new wine in totally new bottles. What they have done, and what the bourgeoisie in nineteenth-century England did with notable success, was to put new wine in old bottles. The high style of the eighteenth-century spectacle survived, but in a new and specialized context. In a variety of ways nineteenth-century consumers were witnessing the modulated transformation of the remnants of the high style into the basic tropes of a new commodity culture.

The Great Exhibition of London:
May 1–October 15, 1851

England and the English on Display

by J.F. Shaw

The world's first international exhibition of consumer goods took place between May 1 and October 15, 1851, in London's Hyde Park. An imposing and impressive glass structure called the Crystal Palace was designed for the event. The Great Exhibition, as the international goods display was called, influenced culture, advertising, art and design education, trade relations, and tourism. It set a precedent for spectacular showcases of manufactured products from all over the world.

The selection that follows represents a contemporary viewpoint on the eve of the Great Exhibition. The author, J.F. Shaw, wrote this piece for a religious periodical in 1851, exhorting the English to behave piously because the eyes of the world will be on England's people as well as its products. He also expresses awe at man's ability, endowed by God, to create impressive consumer goods and to build a structure as remarkable as the Crystal Palace.

The world is growing old. Yet no country has ever had so many foreign eyes looking upon her closely as old England will now have. Eyes that have looked on the snows of Siberia, the forests of Norway, and the vineyards of Spain; on the minarets of Constantinople, and the domes of Rome, and the pyramids of Cairo; on the leisurely flow of the Ganges, the mighty roll of the Amazon, and the tremendous falls of the St. Lawrence; eyes that have watched the lion in tropical forests, and the whale in Polar

J.F. Shaw, *The World's Greatest Assembly*. London: English Monthly Tract Society, 1851.

seas; that have seen the ant-like multitudes of China, and the drear solitudes of African sand; that have witnessed the cannibal festival in Polynesian Isles, and the slave mart on Ethiopian shores, and the carnival in the brilliant cities of Italy, and the gala in the polished capital of France; eyes familiar with every aspect of nature, and every type of religion, and every variety of barbarism, and every grace of civilization, and every stage of art, and every form of government, will soon be busy here gazing upon England.

England Itself Will Be the Exhibition

The politician, eager to ascertain the secret of her stability; the merchant, athirst to find out the springs of her wealth; the patriot, instinct with the ambition of transplanting her freedom; the libertine, resolved to know if the reputed virtue of her homes is only an adroiter mask; the Mussulman [Muslim], who never saw Christianity before, but in its connexion with the worship of images; the Romanist [Roman Catholic], curious to discover the real aspect of Protestantism: presently, all these will have their eyes inquisitively fixed on England, and no doubt will scan and scrutinize the lifesprings of her moral and national existence. The palace of glass will be much, the wonders it contains will be much; but be assured of one thing, that, whatever may be the case with out own countrymen, to all foreigners England and the English will be the great exhibition of 1851.

Never was there a time, when such an assembly as that now gathering on our shore, would have brought with it such an intense curiosity respecting ourselves. Europe has just passed through a frightful series of convulsions, in the midst of which, England has stood erect in hale composure. The attention of all the inquiring men of the age has been fixed on that spectacle. The two great men, whom the first shock of the revolution most directly affected, have both come here, both observed us, both returned to the continent, and published their judgment on the secret of our strength. [F.] Guizot, whom the revolution cast down, and [A.] Lamartine, whom it lifted up, have both told the world that England owes her pre-eminence, which all nations have envied, to her religion. This has not been lost on the active spirits, who, all over the continent, are pondering the great problem, how to make happy their fatherlands. Many of them who never studied religion as a matter of personal salvation, are now studying it as an engine of national improvement. Many of them will look closely to all that indicates the faith we feed upon, and the character which it imparts to us. We shall feel emulous as to the reputation of our artizans; but how little is our real honour involved in a specimen English machine, compared with what it is in a specimen English heart. And every foreigner that peers about our streets, will take each man, of whose character he happens to see any development, as a specimen of what we are. O that all those specimens were such as would either do us honour, or teach them wisdom! But, alas! What scenes will they witness! Our streets by night, our lanes by day, our gin-palaces by night and by day, what testimonies will these utter? Alas! alas! that amid privileges so distinguished, we should have drunkenness reeling before our eyes, and prostitution walking gaily! Then all the worst is sure to be seen. It is the character of vice in English cities, that it is disgustingly conspicuous. A stranger might wander through the streets of Paris for a week, and imagine that he was in a city remarkably correct and blameless. Here our public-houses glare with light; our theatres are opened frequently by the immodest; and the nightly disorder of our streets is undisguised. Thus, the scenes calculated to diminish the moral influence of England, will be universally exhibited. On the other hand, few, very few comparatively, will have any means of looking into families, or of watching, in private life, the operation of christian principles. The scenes calculated to win moral influence for England will be exhibited to few. All who desire to see Europe in repose, and Africa in progress, and Asia in renovation, and America free from the slave stain in the north, and from superstition in the south; all who desire to see christian truth and christian happiness spread throughout the world, must feel that to these ends there is not, at this moment, one single element more important under God, than that the moral influence of England be conserved and augmented. To strengthen our moral influence, is to invigorate every labourer in God's good cause throughout the world; and to impair it, is to enfeeble them all. Englishmen! you have now a great test, and a great opportunity. You will be weighed in the balance of the nations.

Ye that feel the importance of the crisis, be busy with those who do not. Tell the shop-keeper, he must think on our national name, in dealing with our guests. Tell all classes, how reeling intemperance will brand us with the disgrace of inconsistency, before the Romanist of southern Europe, or the Mussulman of the Levant. Teach many, to cry shame on all who would stain the fair fame of

England, in the eye of the stranger. Infuse into the common people a desire to wear gentle manners, and to show rather the courtesy of hosts, than the liberty of scrutineers. Despair not of effecting anything. Purpose a work for the glory of God, for the honour of religion, for the good of mankind; and then, in the Lord's good strength, go forth and do it. You will not wholly fail. You may effect wonders. You shall not work in vain.

Impressing the Stranger

In one great feature of our national life we may hope especially to impress the stranger. It is something for men to see the eager haste of English commerce reined in, and standing mute before the ordinance of God's holy day. It is something for them to see our streets that yesterday teemed with traders, to-day, at one moment hushed and lonely; at another thronged again, but with worshippers now. It is a sight to tell the man who never saw the like, that, There is a God in England. O may that sight move many a heart to remember the Redeemer's cross and shame, and to seek his rest in heaven! But oh! how hatefully do the drinking crowds in the gin-palaces contrast with the assemblies of christian worshippers. And how pitifully do the low markets, in the bye-places, deform the beauty of God's holy day! Remember that your Sabbath is one of the most powerful—ay, perhaps the most powerful—of all the means to be employed, for acquiring moral influence among our visitors. Remember, too, that during their stay, the sanctity of the sabbath will run special risks. And oh! by every sacred motive, urge your neighbours to respect the Lord's day, and call on God to avert, by his own silent ways of working, desecrations and offences. . . .

Here, also, we see men, in great numbers, with tokens at once of Europe and of other realms. They are children of European blood, but of Columbian soil. Sons of the Spaniard, the Portuguese, the Frenchman, and the Anglo-Saxon. But amongst all the vast territories which they divide between them in the new world, those alone that belong to the latter, witness the safety, the light, the order, the progress, and the repose which denote a prosperous State. How strange that, though wise men try to build up a stable policy, on a religion that shuts out God's free word, yet, be it with the absolutism of Italy, or the constitutionalism of Spain, or the republicanism of South America, such nations do not find tranquillity and strength.

But why all this concourse? Why have men left homes so distant and sacrificed their ordinary avocations, and incurred heavy expenses? Why! the man would have little soul indeed, who would not desire to see such a sight as England now presents. When the art of the north and the south, of the west and the east, are to be displayed, who would not be there to gaze and to admire. It is natural, highly natural. And surely one is gladdened to see how all earth's contents are made beautiful or useful by skill. That majestic palace of iron and glass! Awhile ago, its pillars were coarse rude particles, clodded together in some deep recess of the earth, and its transparent plates were sandy masses, without beauty or coherence. How a little fire and a little art have changed them! And these vile bodies that we bear—they, too, may be wonderfully ennobled; and that dust of the dead, around us, what form of more than crystal purity may it not put on, after the great fire that is coming has done its work of renovation. And see how the sand, the clay, the stone—so dull, so cold, by nature—have been transformed into ornaments, that make man's home brilliant, or to uses that make his purpose easy. And the dull metals make sweet music, and the tame wood assumes a hundred admirable positions of service; and the cold of the poles, nurses luxurious furs; and the heat of the equator, fosters delicate silk and versatile cotton; and the elephant sends his ivory; and bird, and fish, and air, and sea, are all ministering to our abundance; and water and fire, yoked to our cars, bear us over the earth, fleet as the wind; and inert metal, marches side by side with Time, echoing in audible tone, its every footfall, and trumpeting the end of every stage. Oh, 'tis indeed wonderful, how God gives man skill to make an inheritance of all things—see the mightiest beasts his docile servants; the most stubborn metals his instrument or his ornament; the winds driving his treasures from the farthest lands; the lightning running his errands; the sea-sand bringing hidden stars up out of the depth to meet his eye; and the poison-plant his medicine. It makes one's heart throb, to see how divine goodness thus endows our human family. But oh! to think of that future state, coming so close upon us, when the sons of God shall indeed "inherit all things", their Father's wisdom and power, calling every element of a new heaven and a new earth, to uncover all its capacity for enriching their pleasures or adorning their homes! Oh! that I may be one of those who share that inheritance; for surely it is pitiful to stand in a world so well replenished as this, and seeing all its abundance, shiver and say, "and I perish of hunger;" but how much more pitiful to open the eye, and behold, far off, the wealth and the joy of the better country, and yet be impoverished for ever,——

Alas! beholding heaven, but feeling hell!

In Awe of the Palace

And as you pass from trophy to trophy, and from wonder to wonder, do you not feel that you would like to see the man that invented this astonishing machine, or executed that wonderful piece of art? It is natural, when you witness an exquisite work, to desire an acquaintance with its author. Wonderful minds, wonderful hands, that planned and wrought these things! Yes, very wonderful. And who planned and made these minds and these hands? If the works of these minds and hands are worth studying, what of the Author of these minds and hands—of the One from whose sole will all this wisdom, and beauty, and power, and order have sprung? Oh! Source of all mind, and skill, and glory, let me know thee! Shut me not out from thy fellowship here, nor deny me hereafter the sight that exceeds all sights—the sight, O matchless God, of thee!

That marvel palace! how splendidly it rose! how wealthily it is stored! how vast and how diversified the throngs that surge around it! And yet, but yesterday that peerless structure was not: and a few short years ago, you might have called throughout all the universe, and of those thoughtful men, those lively women, those sportive children, not one was there to answer. They, too, were not. They have come forth from the hidden depths of the Creator's hand. Yet a little while, and again they will not be. Then, yet a little while, and once more they will come forth, and the nations they belong to, and the fathers that went before them, and the children that shall come after; forth they will stand, multitude on multitude, an array awful exceedingly. And a great white throne, and a King of glory, and ten thousand angels of God, and tromps, and thunders, and dissolving worlds, will make that sight to overpass all the thoughts which rise within us at the expectation of it. And I shall be there to see! Nay, rather to feel; for the interests at stake then, will make me not a spectator, but one involved in the deeds of the day. O God! Three—one, Father, Son, and Holy Ghost, prepare me for that day, and make it a joyful day to me!

Harriet Beecher Stowe's *Uncle Tom's Cabin* Is Published: March 20, 1852

The Influence of Stowe's Novel Is Disputable

by Michael Hanne

In the 1850s, the United States was polarized over the slavery issue. Whether slavery should be permitted or abolished in new and existing states was a controversial political issue in the years leading up to the Civil War (1861–1865). Antislavery reformers and proslavery advocates alike gave zealous expression to their respective views. One of the most passionate and most famous abolitionist works was Harriet Beecher Stowe's novel *Uncle Tom's Cabin, or, Life Among the Lowly.*

Stowe's novel, which condemned the institution of slavery but not the slaveholder, appeared serially in magazine form for eleven months beginning in 1851. Abolitionist John P. Jewett published the novel in book form on March 20, 1852, and over fifty thousand copies were sold in the first two months alone. Three hundred thousand copies were sold the first year and 1 million by the end of the decade. Stage adaptations of the book remained popular for many years. Overall, the novel was well received by abolitionists and frequently denounced by southerners.

In addition to denouncing slavery, Stowe's novel presented a sympathetic portrayal of the slave as a human being. Emphasizing the humanity of the central characters served to underscore the cruelty of the slavery system. Although it is difficult to quantify the influence *Uncle Tom's Cabin* had on the antislavery movement, it is true that the popular novel is one of several events in the 1850s to arouse passionate opinion.

Michael Hanne, in the selection that follows, examines the historical significance of *Uncle Tom's Cabin*. He revisits the 1862 meeting between Harriet Beecher Stowe and President Abraham Lincoln and contrasts Stowe's emphasis on abolition with Lincoln's focus on preserving the Union above all else. Hanne also considers the public reaction to and commentary on Stowe's novel both in the years following its publication and in the twentieth century.

Michael Hanne is professor of comparative literature at Auckland University in New Zealand. In addition to *The Power of the Story: Fiction and Political Change*, he has edited a book on travel writings and has written articles on French and Italian literature.

W hen biographers and literary critics quote Abraham Lincoln's greeting to Harriet Beecher Stowe, "So this is the little lady who made this big war," they almost always interpret it as either a wholly serious or a wholly frivolous comment. In either case they miss the point that the greeting was a tactical shot fired by Lincoln in the context of an ongoing struggle between himself and the advocates of the immediate abolition of slavery.

Stowe Meets President Lincoln

The meeting at which Lincoln is recorded as having spoken these, or similar, words to Stowe occurred in November 1862, just over eighteen months into the Civil War. It was the only occasion on which they ever met. Stowe had thought war unlikely even as late as 1860, but when it did come she welcomed it as a holy crusade against the institution of slavery. In an article of April 1861 in *The Independent*, she wrote: "It is one part of the last struggle for liberty—the American share of the great overturning which shall precede the coming of Him whose right it is—who shall save the poor and needy, and precious shall their blood be in his sight." Her explicitly religious, millenarian conception of American history was distinctly at odds with Lincoln's more secular, pragmatic sense of his historic mission. While he had, since the early 1850s, vigorously opposed the extension of slavery into states in which it was not already established, he had also written, as late as August 1862: "My paramount object in this struggle *is* to save the

Union, and is *not* either to save or destroy slavery. If I could save the Union without freeing *any* slave, I would do it; and if I could save it by freeing *all* the slaves, I would do it; and if I could do it by freeing some and leaving others alone, I would also do that." Nevertheless, only a month later, in September much less ambiguous testimony to the novel's political importance came from many anti-slavery contemporaries of Stowe. Charles Sumner, the abolitionist Massachusetts senator, declared that, without *Uncle Tom's Cabin*, there would have been no Lincoln in the White House. Another abolitionist commentator wrote in 1872 that the novel had been the chief force in developing support for the Republican Party in the 1850s. Frederick Douglass, the black anti-slavery campaigner, stated after the Civil War that Stowe's novel had been "a flash to light a million camp fires in front of the embattled hosts of slavery" (though he also suggested that her role as an activist had been less significant than that of a dozen other women abolitionists). A number of northern historians later in the century argued that the novel had been the most important source of opposition in the North to slavery. James Ford Rhodes was interestingly specific about the mechanisms by which it might have contributed to the building of support for the Republican Party:

> The great influence of Mrs Stowe's book was shown in bringing home to the hearts of the people the conviction that slavery is an injustice; and, indeed, the impression it made upon bearded men was not so powerful as its appeal to women and boys. The mother's opinion was a potent educator in politics between 1852 and 1860, and boys in their teens in the one year were voters in the other. It is often remarked that previous to the war the Republican Party attracted the great majority of the schoolboys, and that the first voters were an important factor in its final success.

Of course all these commentators shared an interest in stressing, as Stowe herself did, the moral, crusading basis of the war. But Southerners, too, and that group of later historians from both North and South who have taken the view that the abolitionists whipped up public opinion in the North toward an unnecessary war, have credited Harriet Beecher Stowe with immense influence—but in order to blame her rather than to pay her tribute. Avery O. Craven, for instance, writing in the early 1940s, stated: "When argument and appeal to reason failed, the abolitionists tried entertainment and appeal to emotion. *Uncle Tom's Cabin . . .* became a best seller in the most complete sense. Only the Bible exceeded it in numbers sold and in the thoroughness with which it was read in England and America." (It is unanimously accepted that *Uncle Tom's Cabin* reached a massive white readership, in every social class, even including people who otherwise read very little, and that some of the most unlikely readers admitted to being moved by it. In ten months between 1852 and 1853, it sold an astonishing 300,000 copies in the United States alone, and, within a year, two-and-a-half million copies around the world. As Elizabeth Ammons has recently expressed 1862, he had decided that, to relieve pressure from the abolitionists within his Republican Party (and to preempt foreign intervention in the war), it would be expedient to issue the Emancipation Proclamation.

In November 1862, Harriet Beecher Stowe, the most famous woman in America following the publication of *Uncle Tom's Cabin* in book form ten years before, was preparing an article on the war for a British women's magazine. She wanted to argue that the whole purpose of the war, as far as the North was concerned, was to free the slaves and that Britain should therefore, on moral grounds, support the Union. But it was still not clear how seriously the Proclamation was to be taken. So she went to Washington in November, "to satisfy myself that I may refer to the Emancipation Proclamation as a reality and a substance not to fizzle out at the little end of the horn as I should be sorry to call the attention of my sisters in Europe to any such impotent conclusion . . . I mean to have a talk with 'Father Abraham' himself among others." The President would have known very well that Harriet Beecher Stowe was going to press him on the seriousness of his intentions concerning emancipation, as every other abolitionist at that period did.

Lincoln's greeting to Stowe was not, then, an affirmation that abolitionism in general, let alone Harriet Beecher Stowe in particular, had been primarily responsible for bringing about the Civil War. It was a provocative quip, and by making it Lincoln acknowledged the extraordinary manner in which, over the preceding ten years, the question of the political and economic interests of the Union, with which Lincoln was preoccupied, had become intertwined with the moral and religious issues relating to slavery, which the abolitionists had been pressing for so long. It was a reluctant admission that the Union cause could not do without the abolitionists, yet, at the same time, a polite reminder that the abolitionists would never have brought the nation to the threshold of emancipation without the political, economic, and military pragmatism of the Republican Party. The meeting between Lincoln and Stowe epitomized the curious blend, not only of different human motives, but of contrasting emplotments of historical narrative embraced by the different parties in the North who were committed to the war. . . .

Praise and Criticism

If Lincoln's words to Stowe constituted only a limited and grudging acknowledgement of the role played by *Uncle Tom's Cabin* in preparing public opinion for a war between North and South, in part over slavery, it, "her novel riveted the nation . . . kept the printing presses running night and day, making grown men weep and preachers rail."

Modern Interpretations of the Novel's Significance

In [the twentieth] century, there has been a tendency to downplay, in one way or another, the causal link between *Uncle Tom's Cabin* and the war and emancipation. This has resulted partly from a sensible trend towards acknowledging the multiplicity of factors which contributed to the Civil War, with the issue of slavery being viewed as only one element in the clash between an agrarian culture in the South and a rapidly modernizing, industrial culture in the North, a conflict which as a consequence of institutional deficiencies and the personal failings of the political leaders of the time was not resolved before war became inevitable. But the belittling of the influence of *Uncle Tom's Cabin* also reflects ongoing struggles in the United States over race, gender, and the social function of literature.

Mainstream critics, mostly white, male, and formed in the tradition of the New Criticism, have generally written in a dismissively patronizing way of Stowe's work. This is partly due to their insistence on detaching literature from the hurly-burly of political life, raising it to a distinct, no doubt higher, realm of its own. An article in a major history of American literature is typical in asserting that "in spite of the enormous vogue of Mrs Stowe's novel, it is doubtful if a book ever had much power to change the course of events." But it is also part of a very successful attempt, until quite recently, to marginalize and trivialize the whole tradition of sentimental novels by women to which *Uncle Tom's Cabin* belongs. The same article concludes with the astonishing comment that "obviously Harriet Beecher Stowe was neither a great personality nor a great artist."

Recent criticism of *Uncle Tom's Cabin* by African-American and feminist commentators has not so much denied its contribution to the coming of war and emancipation as cut across that claim with other sorts of claims. African-American writers have emphasized the reactionary, racist features of the novel: the destructive, limiting stereotypes of black passivity (in the case of Uncle Tom) and foolish clowning (of Sam and Andy on the Shelby estate, Topsy in the St. Clare household, and other minor slave characters) which it has offered black and white readers in the century and more since the Civil War. As Richard Yarborough has expressed it, "although Stowe unquestionably sympathized with the slaves, her commitment to challenging the claim of black inferiority was frequently undermined by her own endorsement of racial stereotypes." They have also lamented Stowe's enthusiastic reiteration of the colonizationist argument: that blacks, once freed, would prefer to leave the United States, because they did not feel it was *their* country, for a nation of their own in Africa, especially Liberia: "Heavenly salvation might indeed be possible for blacks but a truly just interracial society was inconceivable." James Baldwin's devastating attack on *Uncle Tom's Cabin*, in an essay entitled "Everybody's Protest Novel," implies that, even if it did contribute to emancipation, it would have been better, in the long term for blacks, if this "very bad novel" had never been written. While there is very little doubt that, for almost a century *after* the Civil War, the existence of *Uncle Tom's Cabin* (and especially the numerous crudely reactionary stage adaptations of the novel) served almost entirely the forces obstructing black aspirations, this does not affect the seriousness of claims for its contribution to emancipation and the war.

10 Harriet Beecher Stowe's *Uncle Tom's Cabin* Is Published: March 20, 1852

Slavery Dehumanizes the Slave

by Harriet Beecher Stowe

The antislavery novel *Uncle Tom's Cabin, or, Life Among the Lowly* by Harriet Beecher Stowe was an immediate best seller upon its publication in March 1852. Stowe was inspired in part by the Fugitive Slave Law of 1850. This law permitted slave owners to recapture and punish escaped slaves, even if the escapees had reached a free state. Stowe, who had previously shown little concern with the antislavery movement, decided to write a novel that condemned the institution of slavery.

There are two story lines in the novel. Mr. Shelby, a Kentucky plantation owner, plans to settle a debt by selling two of his slaves. One is Uncle Tom, who is intelligent, pious, and respected. The other is a young boy, but the boy's mother (Eliza) and her husband (George Harris) escape with the boy to the North. The novel then traces the paths of each of these characters, and along the way the slave's humanity—a topic often overlooked by other writers—emerges.

The following excerpt from *Uncle Tom's Cabin* reveals the novel's emotional tone. Miss Ophelia, cousin to deceased slave owner Augustine St. Clare, tries to persuade Marie (St. Clare's widow) to free Tom. Tom's freedom was among the last wishes of St. Clare, but Marie refuses to acquiesce and chooses to sell him instead. Next, the novel introduces the reader to the slave warehouse where Tom is to be sold. Stowe beckons the reader to consider the

---

Harriet Beecher Stowe, *Uncle Tom's Cabin*. Columbus, OH: Charles E. Merrill, 1969.

nature of a market that sells human beings, and describes the noisy atmosphere there that is intended to distract the slaves from reflecting upon their lot.

"There's one thing I wanted to speak with you about," said Miss Ophelia. "Augustine promised Tom his liberty, and began the legal forms necessary to it. I hope you will use your influence to have it perfected."

"Indeed, I shall do no such thing!" said Marie, sharply.

Marie had her face covered with her handkerchief at this appeal, and began sobbing and using her smelling-bottle, with great vehemence.

"Everybody goes against me!" she said. "Everybody is so inconsiderate! I shouldn't have expected that *you* would bring up all these remembrances of my troubles to me,—it's so inconsiderate! But nobody ever does consider,—my trials are so peculiar! It's so hard, that when I had only one daughter, she should have been taken!—and when I had a husband that just exactly suited me,— and I'm so hard to be suited!—he should be taken! And you seem to have so little feeling for me, and keep bringing it up to me so carelessly,—when you know how it overcomes me! I suppose you mean well; but it is very inconsiderate,—very!" And Marie sobbed, and gasped for breath, and called Mammy to open the window, and to bring her the camphor-bottle, and to bathe her head, and unhook her dress. And, in the general confusion that ensued, Miss Ophelia made her escape to her apartment.

She saw, at once, that it would do no good to say anything more; for Marie had an indefinite capacity for hysteric fits; and, after this, whenever her husband's or Eva's wishes with regard to the servants were alluded to, she always found it convenient to set one in operation. Miss Ophelia, therefore, did the next best thing she could for Tom,—she wrote a letter to Mrs. Shelby for him, stating his troubles, and urging them to send to his relief.

Marched to the Slave-Warehouse

The next day, Tom and Adolph, and some half a dozen other servants, were marched down to a slave-warehouse, to await the convenience of the trader, who was going to make up a lot for auction. . . .

"Tom is one of the most valuable servants on the place,—it

couldn't be afforded, any way. Besides, what does he want of liberty? He's a great deal better off as he is."

"But he does desire it, very earnestly, and his master promised it," said Miss Ophelia.

"I dare say he does want it," said Marie; "they all want it, just because they are a discontented set,—always wanting what they haven't got. Now, I'm principled against emancipating, in any case. Keep a negro under the care of a master, and he does well enough, and is respectable; but set them free, and they get lazy, and won't work, and take to drinking, and go all down to be mean, worthless fellows. I've seen it tried, hundreds of times. It's no favor to set them free."

"But Tom is so steady, industrious, and pious."

"O, you needn't tell me! I've seen a hundred like him. He'll do very well, as long as he's taken care of,—that's all."

"But, then, consider," said Miss Ophelia, "when you set him up for sale, the chances of his getting a bad master."

"O, that's all humbug!" said Marie; "it isn't one time in a hundred that a good fellow gets a bad master; most masters are good, for all the talk that is made. I've lived and grown up here, in the South, and I never yet was acquainted with a master that didn't treat his servants well,—quite as well as is worth while. I don't feel any fears on that head."

"Well," said Miss Ophelia, energetically, "I know it was one of the last wishes of your husband that Tom should have his liberty; it was one of the promises that he made to dear little Eva [Marie and Augustine St. Clare's daughter] on her death-bed, and I should not think you would feel at liberty to disregard it."

A SLAVE warehouse! Perhaps some of my readers conjure up horrible visions of such a place. They fancy some foul, obscure den, some horrible *Tartarus "informis, ingens, cui lumen ademptum."* But no, innocent friend; in these days men have learned the art of sinning expertly and genteelly, so as not to shock the eyes and senses of respectable society. Human property is high in the market and is, therefore, well fed, well cleaned, tended, and looked after, that it may come to sale sleek, and strong, and shining. A slave-warehouse in New Orleans is a house externally not much unlike many others, kept with neatness; and where every day you may see arranged, under a sort of shed along the outside, rows of men and women, who stand there as a sign of the property sold within.

Then you shall be courteously entreated to call and examine, and shall find an abundance of husbands, wives, brothers, sisters, fathers, mothers, and young children, to be "sold separately, or in lots to suit the convenience of the purchaser;" and that soul immortal, once bought with blood and anguish by the Son of God, when the earth shook, and the rocks rent, and the graves were opened, can be sold, leased, mortgaged, exchanged for groceries or dry goods, to suit the phases of trade, or the fancy of the purchaser.

Noisy Mirth to Drown Reflection

It was a day or two after the conversation between Marie and Miss Ophelia, that Tom, Adolph, and about half a dozen others of the St. Clare estate, were turned over to the loving kindness of Mr. Skeggs, the keeper of a depot on————street, to await the auction, next day.

Tom had with him quite a sizable trunk full of clothing, as had most others of them. They were ushered, for the night, into a long room, where many other men, of all ages, sizes, and shades of complexion, were assembled, and from which roars of laughter and unthinking merriment were proceeding. "Ah, ha! that's right. Go it, boys,—go it!" said Mr. Skeggs, the keeper. "My people are always so merry! Sambo, I see!" he said, speaking approvingly to a burly negro who was performing tricks of low buffoonery, which occasioned the shouts which Tom had heard.

As might be imagined, Tom was in no humor to join these proceedings; and, therefore, setting his trunk as far as possible from the noisy group, he sat down on it, and leaned his face against the wall.

The dealers in the human article make scrupulous and systematic efforts to promote noisy mirth among them, as a means of drowning reflection, and rendering them insensible to their condition. The whole object of the training to which the negro is put, from the time he is sold in the northern market till he arrives south, is systematically directed towards making him callous, unthinking, and brutal. The slave-dealer collects his gang in Virginia or Kentucky, and drives them to some convenient, healthy place,— often a watering place,—to be fattened. Here they are fed full daily; and, because some incline to pine, a fiddle is kept commonly going among them, and they are made to dance daily; and he who refuses to be merry—in whose soul thoughts of wife, or child, or home, are too strong for him to be gay—is marked as sullen and dangerous, and subjected to all the evils which the ill will of an utterly irresponsible and hardened man can inflict upon him. Briskness, alertness, and cheerfulness of appearance, especially before observers, are constantly enforced upon them, both by the hope of thereby getting a good master, and the fear of all that the driver may bring upon them, if they prove unsalable.

11 Commodore Perry "Opens" Japan: July 14, 1853

The United States Reaches Across the Pacific

by Charles E. Neu

By the mid–nineteenth century, the westward expansion of the United States was in full force, and this push west piqued Americans' curiosity in East Asia. The possibilities of a connection with Japan, which over the course of several centuries had cultivated a self-imposed isolation from diplomatic relations and world affairs, appealed to the American government. In 1852, Commodore Matthew Perry embarked on a government-sanctioned expedition to "open" Japan; that is, his aim was to establish formal U.S.-Japanese relations. He carried with him a letter from President Millard Fillmore that, it was hoped, would facilitate diplomacy.

Fillmore's letter addressed several issues of diplomatic significance to the United States, including requests for a way station in the Japanese islands, for trading privileges in Japanese ports, and for protection of American whalers working in the northern Pacific Ocean.

The initial response of the Japanese to the Perry expedition was disdain and diffidence. Eventually, though, Perry was invited to set foot on land. On July 14, 1853, two Japanese officials ceremoniously accepted Fillmore's letter, marking the start of a diplomatic relationship between the two countries.

The following selection by Charles E. Neu explains both the origins of the impetus toward U.S.-Japan relations, the prevailing opin-

Charles E. Neu, *Troubled Encounter: The United States and Japan.* New York: John Wiley & Sons, 1975. Copyright © 1975 by John Wiley & Sons, Inc. All rights reserved. Reproduced by permission.

ions about East Asia, and the effects of Perry's mission. Neu describes Perry's own attitude toward the expedition and his reception upon his return to the United States.

Charles E. Neu is professor emeritus of American history at Brown University. He is the author of numerous books and specializes in the study of U.S. relations with East Asia.

H eightened interest in Japan took place against the backdrop of the 1840s, a decade that brought a culmination of expansionist fervor. It was a decade of confidence and ambition, full of frantic activity and of the exuberance of a people on the move, fascinated by what [poet] Walt Whitman described as the "enormous untravelled plains and forests" of the West. Imaginations soared as men contemplated the glorious destiny of their nation. America now stood, so it seemed to men at the time, at the center of Western civilization, on the cutting edge of progress. Commerce thrived, geographical barriers vanished, and the vision of a republic stretching from the Atlantic to the Pacific became commonplace. Often, however, it was a troubled vision, for many in the North already believed, as Senator William H. Seward proclaimed, that slavery was "incompatible with all . . . the elements of the security, welfare, and greatness of nations." The bitter contention surrounding the Mexican War revealed the depth of these feelings and the way in which they could become entangled with aspects of continental expansion. Nevertheless, the nation moved west and, by the end of the decade, gazed across the Pacific. . . .

An Expansionist Mood

By the late 1840s a shift had begun to occur in American perceptions of the outside world. The United States had achieved a large trade in the Atlantic, and now East Asia beckoned more strongly than ever before [American author] Herman Melville caught the popular curiosity when he wrote of "unknown Archipelagoes and impenetrable Japans." To some missionaries, naval officers, and adventurers, East Asia seemed more challenging than areas in which the American presence was older and better established. Japan in particular seemed a mysterious archipelago, a land of paradox. Filled with an intelligent and frugal people, it was governed by a cruel despotism, one that practiced barbarism, duplicity, and treachery. This image of Japan aroused the intense curiosity of some Americans. Moreover, the acquisition of new Pacific Coast possessions, the development of isthmian routes, and the talk of a transcontinental railway exalted expansionists who had for decades dreamed of making the American West the passage to India. Senator Thomas Hart Benton believed that "the European merchant, as well as the American, will fly across our continent on a straight line to China," while Secretary of the Treasury Robert J. Walker claimed that "Asia has suddenly become our neighbor with a placid, intervening ocean inviting our steamships upon the track of a commerce greater than that of all Europe combined."

By the middle of the nineteenth century, then, changes in the expansionist mood gave a new impetus to a Japan expedition. While many Americans felt that duty compelled the United States to open Japan to the commerce and civilization of the West, more specific interests also urged an American expedition. Naval officers hoped to win prestige for themselves and their nation; the American whaling industry wanted ports of refuge and protection for shipwrecked seamen; some commercial interests, impressed by the growth of the China trade in the 1840s, dwelled on the commercial possibilities of Japan; and those determined to establish a Pacific steamship line to China believed that Japan, with its allegedly rich coal deposits, would be an essential stopping point. In Congress, too, agitation grew. Although only a handful of men actively pushed for it, many felt, as the *Democratic Review* put it, that "the opening of commerce with Japan is demanded by reason, civilization, progress and religion." It was no surprise when, in early 1851, President Millard Fillmore decided to send a naval force to Japan to secure "friendship, commerce, a supply of coal and provisions, and protection for our shipwrecked people."

Perry's Vision of America's Destiny

The President's aims were modest. He saw the end of Japanese isolation as a way to enlarge peacefully both American prestige and commerce in East Asia. Although the area was of peripheral concern, he wished for the expedition's success and took great care in the selection of its commander, Matthew C. Perry. Commodore Perry had developed some interest in the Pacific after the Mexican War, but he agreed to assume command of the East India Squadron only after assurances by the administration that he would preside over a sizable force with ample funds for equipment and gifts. Once committed to the enterprise, Perry prepared for it with vigor. He talked with whalers at New Bedford, read Europeanbooks on Japan, and concluded that only an ominous display of force combined with a haughty, distant attitude would bring success. Perry viewed the Japanese as "weak and semi-barbarous," "deceitful," and "vindictive in character." In dealing with them, the ordinary rules of discourse among civilized peoples did not apply. Only extraordinary measures would convince their rulers to receive the President's letter and to grant American demands. Perry was far less reluctant than the President to use force to achieve these ends and far more conscious of past humiliations inflicted on American vessels by the Japanese government.

Perry's leadership endowed the expedition with a loftier purpose than the Fillmore administration had intended. Already a fervent advocate of Manifest Destiny, he came to view the opening of Japan as the great object of his life and proclaimed the inevitability of American expansion into the Pacific. Predicting an Anglo-American struggle for control of that ocean, Perry sought strategic outposts to strengthen America's position. His wide discretionary powers and the slowness of communications provided many opportunities to pursue these larger aims.

When Perry reached the Pacific in the spring of 1853, he began to act on his broad vision of the nation's destiny. He visited the Ryūkyūs and the Bonins, forced concessions from the rulers of those islands, and even contemplated the bases that both island chains could provide for America's Pacific empire. On July 8 his four "black ships" arrived in what is today the Bay of Tokyo (then Edo Bay), prepared for determined resistance from the Japanese. Perry decided, as he had done years before at Naples, to make his demands and depart, promising to return with a more imposing force. But, before leaving, Perry intimidated the Japanese by moving his ships closer to Tokyo, the capital of the Tokugawa Shogunate, than any other foreign vessels had dared to advance. Purposefully remote and sensitive to the slightest affronts to his dignity, he finally brought his first visit to a culmination by delivering the President's letter to Japanese authorities in an elaborate ceremony on the shores of Tokyo Bay. Full of a sense of historic purpose, he wrote in his journal that "we pray God that our present attempt to bring a singular and isolated people into the family of civilized nations may succeed without bloodshed."

In March 1854 Perry returned to Japan with an enlarged squadron to negotiate the Treaty of Kanagawa. His tactics were typical of the era. He warned the Japanese of the fate of Mexico, threatened to assemble an even larger force, and made it clear that he intended to achieve his aims at whatever cost. Despite his bluster, however, Perry dropped his demand for commercial relations and settled for a treaty that provided for the protection of the crews of shipwrecked vessels, the opening of two ports where American ships could obtain coal, wood, water and supplies, and the right to station consular officials in these ports. Perry knew that he had made only a small beginning, but he confidently expected others to carry forward the great work that he had launched.

Mixed Feelings Toward Asia

Perry's belligerency and desire for territorial aggrandizement worried the American government and brought out what was to become a persistent dichotomy in American East Asian policy. Most American diplomats in China and Japan were restless and impatient, inspired by a vision of an American empire of commerce and religion in East Asia. As men on the spot, they were influenced by the course of events and by the attitudes of their European colleagues. Their activism contrasted sharply with the passivity of their government. More often than not, the American government was indifferent to their needs and programs; officials in Washington had a far narrower vision of American interests in East Asia. The government negotiated treaties to open China and Japan to Western influence and to encourage the growth of commerce. But these objectives, once achieved, satisfied leaders in Washington, who wished to avoid further involvement. When difficulties arose over commercial rights and the protection of missionaries and other Westerners, the United States usually responded cautiously. In the 1850s events in Japan temporarily obscured the fact that in East Asia the United States was a minor power, without the resources or the will to sustain major policy initiatives. For men in Washington, as for most Americans, Asia remained an abstract idea, a distant area that was only one part of a worldwide commercial empire. American representatives in China and Japan seldom shared this attitude and, because of the lag in communications, often pursued their private goals.

Full of grandiose objectives in East Asia, Perry was inevitably disappointed on his return to the United States in early 1855. He received a warm but not overwhelming reception, and the Democratic administration of Franklin Pierce seemed cool toward

Perry's elaborate vision of the nation's Pacific destiny. Perry proclaimed that the Treaty of Kanagawa was "a mere commencement" in "bringing a mighty Empire into the family of nations and within the influence of our benign religion." The government did, to be sure, follow up Perry's achievement with the dispatch of Townsend Harris as the first American consul in Japan but, by this time, the nation's leaders were absorbed in more pressing foreign and domestic problems.

American interest in East Asia—which peaked during the 1840s and early 1850s—began to wane. The lure of Asia had always been a subordinate theme in American expansionism, serving as one of many justifications for the conquest of the continent. Those who saw the American West more as a bridge to Asia than as an area to be settled and developed in its own right were understandably excited by the vistas unveiled by expansion to the Pacific and the opening of Japan. For most Americans, however, the vision of the American West as a passage to India was never the central motive for the westward movement and became even less compelling in the 1850s as they turned more decisively inward. Gradually the American people had grasped the potential resources and enormous dimensions of the West. The acquisition of California and Oregon, although it gave a brief impetus to the thrust into East Asia, presented Americans with the reality of a continental empire and coalesced feelings about the abundance of the West. It brought a shift of consciousness as men began to think, far more than previously, in terms of a great internal, landed empire to be peopled and tamed. The theme of the West as a passage to India gave way to the theme of the West as the "garden of the world," a vast, interior space that would shape the promise and define the meaning of American life.

11 Commodore Perry "Opens" Japan: July 14, 1853

Perry Meets the Japanese Delegates

by Wilhelm Heine

In 1851 Commodore Matthew Perry sent a memorandum to the secretary of the navy, proposing a show of naval strength that, Perry suggested, could result in friendly American-Japanese relations. For centuries Japan had been closed diplomatically to the United States and other nations, and Perry's idea won government officials' favor. Perry, who did not want to command the expedition but accepted the commission anyway, departed from Norfolk, Virginia, on November 24, 1852. The flagship *Missouri* and three other ships made the journey to Edo (Tokyo) Bay and dropped anchor there on July 2, 1853. After several inconsequential demands to meet with Japanese officials, Perry was finally invited ashore to present his letter on July 14.

These events are described in the following excerpt from a memoir by Wilhelm Heine, who accompanied Perry on the expedition to Japan. Heine was a native of Dresden, Germany, and eventually became an American citizen. He taught painting in Europe and the United States prior to the Perry expedition, which he chronicled in words, drawings, and paintings. In the selection that follows, Heine depicts in great detail the meeting on July 14. His account conveys the sights, sounds, and mood of the ceremonious encounter. He closes by noting that the meeting went well and that Perry announced his intention to return to Japan in twelve months to finalize a treaty.

Wilhelm Heine, *With Perry to Japan: A Memoir*, translated by Frederic Trautmann. Honolulu: University of Hawaii Press, 1990.

This morning, the twelfth [14 July 1853], we saw a medley of flags decorating the batteries and forts. Long sheets of black-and-white cloth had been stretched inside the walls. Earlier travelers, discussing these sheets installed above the guns, assumed that they served to conceal the armed interior below. Our interpreter, Mr. Wells Williams, did not agree. (He and Dr. [Peter] Parker passed along these coasts sixteen years earlier [as missionaries] in the *Morrison* from Canton.) He thought that the sheets, erected close together, were to protect the cannoneers from rifle bullets. To me, this interpretation seemed the better one. For, however ineffective against bombardment, they would be of some value as a screen against small arms.

Ready for Reception

At about 8:00 A.M. the governor of Uraga and several officials came aboard with an announcement. Everything was ready for the reception ashore, they said. This time each Japanese wore full dress: something like baggy trousers of heavy black silk, ankle-length, held up by strips of silk like our suspenders, and hemmed generously, top and bottom, in dark blue silk; a close-fitting sleeved vest or jacket, of silk, tucked into the top of the trousers; around the waist the usual belt and the pair of swords; and over the whole a kind of cloak like the Spanish poncho or our Catholic priest's surplice except for the slit down the front and the clasp to hold the halves together. Cloaks differed according to wearer's rank: for higher ranks, a heavy silk, woven like brocade, in gold, silver, and [other] colors; for the lower, a nondescript fabric, usually red but occasionally yellow. All cloaks, regardless of wearer's rank, were edged and hemmed with gold and silver and coats of arms embroidered on the shoulders and across the chest.

At 9:00 A.M. the call to boats sounded—after some ships had anchored opposite the meeting place. From there, should worst come to worst for us [ashore], they could protect us with their cannon. Fifteen boats took four hundred men from the several ships. Shortly before 10:00 A.M. the *Susquehanna*'s gun announced the commodore's departure. The flotilla of boats set off for the rendezvous about two miles west of Uraga, in a small inlet. The village of Kurihama lay on the inlet.

About 150 [Japanese] boats ringed the inlet. We saw a group of richly dressed officials in front of two spacious pavilions that had been erected ashore. To the right and left, sheets of black cloth had been stretched at a height of six to eight feet for about two miles. Units of soldiers ranged along them. The number of soldiers could not be readily estimated, their formation being ragged and ill-defined. The Japanese announced six thousand; it had to be at least five thousand. Most carried spear or musket, others bow and arrow; but all the ubiquitous pair of swords. Why *two?* I see no reason except pomp: mere show.

About 150 soldiers, armed with muskets and bayoneted rifles, had been arrayed near the pavilions, in two ranks, military style, weapons at the order. The rest of the soldiers formed irregular groups here and there. Two cannon on the left flank, three- or four-pounders, in bronze and on carriages of ancient vintage, looked like old Spanish or Portuguese. They probably dated from the Japanese war of extermination against Portuguese Christians. Officers of the various units sat on low seats, each under his unit's insignia. Orderlies, behind the ranks, held a number of horses of small breed but strong and well built: their saddles, harness, and trappings showy and inlaid abundantly with silver and gold; manes cut short; and tails brightly decorated, sometimes enclosed in a container of vivid fabric, sometimes entwined with pieces of colored cloth. When our band played, the horses pricked up their ears, cut hoof-stomping caprioles, and caused disturbances among the soldiers. Other soldiers, carrying pikes of various shapes and fifteen to sixteen feet long, did nothing but keep close, a few to each horse.

Four companies of ours, two of marines and two of sailors, had formed where the commodore would land, marines right, sailors left. Two bands—one of marines, one of sailors—provided music in addition to the usual complement of red-jacketed drummers and fifers. A major [Jacob Zeilin] and a captain [William B. Slack] commanded the marines; four lieutenants and two midshipmen, the sailors. The remaining officers, about forty (the commodore's staff), awaited the commodore himself at the spot where he would debark.

Setting Foot on Land

The moment the commodore set foot on land, the governor of Uraga and his entourage appeared. (The governor had arrived a little earlier.) He welcomed everybody, and then the grand procession started for the pavilions, not far off.

Long sheets of black and white formed a kind of outer courtyard. Japanese and Americans stayed outside it except the governor and a small retinue and the commodore and a small staff. Each leader thus left most of his followers behind.

The governor escorted the commodore into the courtyard, across mats that had been laid there, and up several steps to the open adjoining pavilion. The imperial councilors—Toda, prince of Idsu, and Ido, prince of Iwami—waited in the pavilion. Toda sat a bit higher than Ido. To Ido's right another official kneeled [until we drew near], Yezaimon, whose rank I was unable to learn. He, the governor of Uraga, and the interpreter Tatsonoske bowed deeply before Prince Toda, kneeled there, and remained kneeling throughout [the day's] negotiations. The commodore and the senior captains were asked to take the three seats of equal height opposite Toda's. The other American officers gathered behind the commodore. The rest of the governor's retinue stayed in the courtyard, kneeling.

We had been told that these were imperial representatives of the highest rank. In the lives of their people ceremony and formality took precedence over everything else. The councilors' underlings always removed their shoes upon entry and, when speaking to the councilors, kneeled and touched their foreheads continually to the ground. Dutch and Russian emissaries in Japan before us had been compelled to disgraceful humiliation. And now we entered with such little ado, and we remained erect.

What an outlandish and insolent spectacle we therefore presented to the Japanese. How different our behavior from that of the Russians and the Dutch, what a lurid contrast our manner against that of the councilors' underlings, and how egregious we alien barbarians must have seemed to the councilors. Perhaps the Dutch and Russian emissaries had been instructed to respond with obeisance to every impudent Japanese policeman and to kneel and crawl, backward and forward, time after time. Not so with us, thank God! The commodore had made up his mind; no disgraceful humiliation would be inflicted on *him.*

Accordingly he issued the strictest of orders, and we paid each Japanese the courtesy that would have been paid a man of his position in the United States. This policy produced obviously excellent results. Yes, the Japanese sycophants at first looked askance. But they took comfort at last when they saw aboard ship that our officers enjoyed respect and that each subordinate obeyed every command with prompt assent—all without shameful subservience and servile formalities. The Japanese also observed that we received their representatives aboard and, without degrading ourselves, treated them with cordiality and warmth.

True, the Japanese had objected to our survey of the bay and to our anchoring wherever it suited us. They had tried to justify their gestures of resistance: "You have contradicted the wishes of our government, and we must do as we are told." But we retorted: "We are honoring the wishes of *our* government, and *we* must do as *we* are told. Besides, we are accustomed to behave this way all over the world. So we shall behave this way here, too!" We also declared, however, and at the same time, that the United States felt nothing but friendship for Japan. At any rate, the Japanese could do nothing but comply, though our actions be new to them. For, in the end, small boats and twelve-pound cannon would have been a squeak against the roar of our mighty steamships and heavy artillery.

Perry Will Return

The Japanese again showed the commodore the document that vested imperial authority in them. The commodore responded with his diplomatic credentials and the letter for the emperor from the president. Each of these documents bore the Great Seal of the United States in a dangling gold skippet. The two handsomest cabin boys brought them forward, each in its container: a case with a golden clasp and a golden lock. After the cases were opened, a short speech set forth the purpose of the commodore's mission. Then the documents—and translations of them into Dutch, Chinese, and French—were presented to the imperial councilors, and they accepted them. The documents were then placed with much ceremony in a roomy chest, and the chest shut, locked, wrapped many times with a stout cord of silk, and tied with an array of astounding knots.

"No doubt," the commodore added at the end of the meeting, "mature deliberation will have to take place on my mission and my message. Therefore I shall leave now and return in the spring." Again the Japanese were seeing and hearing what they had never seen or heard before. The commodore behaved nothing like the emissaries of other nations who had preceded him. Those unfortunates had waited long months in ignominious semi-imprisonment until it pleased the Japanese to answer them equivocally and let them go at last.

"I shall leave, I shall return," the commodore had announced. The Japanese made no bones about it; the announcement astounded them. Then Perry explained that the awesome military power [of our ships], so close to the imperial capital, could give rise to incorrect assumptions. "I do not want in the least to influence discussions." As an act of politeness, therefore, we will go away, he said, and the Japanese calmed down.

Everyone exchanged courtesies in farewell and left the pavilion. We embarked in good order. For Major [Jacob] Z[eilin] had gone to the marines and assembled the drums and fifes, and we got into the boats to a famous old tune. It had never been heard on the shores of Nippon, but now, with drums obbligato, "Yankee Doodle" rang out—to the delight of all.

The governor and his officials accompanied us to the ships and came aboard. They behaved with the reserve of people who think it indecorous to let one's curiosity show. Yet they studied everything below; it had been out of their sight until now. The ship's machinery, the heavy cannons and their percussion locks, the rifles, the revolvers—that sort of thing provoked the greatest astonishment. On the other hand, familiar with maps of the earth and charts of the heavens, they pointed out—on the globe and with precision—not only Japan, Russia, England, Holland, and the United States but their capitals and other features. And they asked a variety of questions, indicating considerable knowledge of international affairs.

"Does Mexico still exist? Or has the United States conquered it by now?"

"Has the giant railroad been built from New York to San Francisco, really?"

On and on, question after question. With each, a finger went—correctly—to the place meant.

We received numerous gifts before we departed: fabrics (including gold brocade), over a hundred fowls, over a thousand eggs, all sorts of lacquerware, saki, fans, and other things. The commodore responded with gifts. Politely the Japanese declined the several valuable arms and weapons. But wines, jams, preserves, and candied fruits seemed all the more welcome; the Japanese enjoyed them aboard whenever possible. Especially on the last day, when champagne flowed and Uraga's lord governor and suite left in uncommonly good humor.

The Crimean War Brought Change and Innovation

by A.J. Barker

Mid-nineteenth-century Europe underwent significant political change. Although the revolutions of 1848 fostered liberalism and nationalism, many effects—such as Italy's unification, Germany's unification, and Russia's emancipation of serfs—did not occur until later in the century. A catalyst of these later developments was the Crimean War, between Russia and an alliance of the (Turkish) Ottoman Empire, Great Britain, and France.

The declining Ottoman Empire, dubbed the "sick man of Europe" in the mid–nineteenth century, was at the center of the conflict in the Crimea, a region on the Black Sea. Two issues were the immediate cause of war. The first was whether Western Latin Christians, or Orthodox Christians, would control the holy sites places in Jerusalem. The Ottoman Empire granted this honor to (Western Latin) France, and (Orthodox) Russia disputed the gesture. Second, Russia wanted control over Ottoman provinces in what is now Romania. Russia occupied two such provinces in summer 1853; within several months the Ottoman Empire declared war on Russia. The war became one between major European states when Great Britain and France, in opposition to Russian expansion, declared war on the czar's empire on March 28, 1854.

The war's decisive battle came in September 1855 with the fall of the Russian fortress of Sevastopol. Peace negotiations began shortly

A.J. Barker, *The Vainglorious War: 1854–1856*. London: Weidenfeld and Nicolson, 1970.

thereafter, with France as the dominant diplomatic power, and concluded in March 1856 with the signing of the Peace of Paris. By the terms of the treaty, Russia had to surrender territory and not interfere in the affairs of the Ottoman Empire's Orthodox Christians. The Crimean War also dissolved the Concert of Europe, an 1815 instrument designed to resolve foreign policy disputes among Russia, Great Britain, Austria, and Prussia. Without this agency, European nations increasingly based foreign and domestic policy decisions on self-interest. Unification in Italy and Germany and the emancipation of the serfs in Russia resulted.

In the selection that follows, A.J. Barker examines the causes and consequences of the Crimean War. He discusses the confidence and impetus for aggression of the Russian czar [Nicholas I]. Barker also addresses British and French motivations for entering the war. In addition, Barker lists Crimean War innovations, such as increased use of shells and rifles, as well as the first use of the telegraph in a war.

British historian A.J. Barker is the author of over twelve books on wars and warfare in the nineteenth and twentieth centuries.

N ever had the prestige of a Tsar stood higher than that of Nicholas I in the summer of 1853. Five years earlier a revolutionary tide had rolled across Europe, sweeping Louis-Philippe off the throne of France, causing the Emperor of Austria to flee from his capital, King Frederick IV of Prussia to leave Berlin, Hungary to break away from Austria and provoking Italy's revolt against Habsburg rule. Nicholas had come to the rescue, effectively intervening on behalf of his neighbours and using his army to crush the Hungarian insurrectionists. Nicholas was taking no chances with liberal movements; he stood for stability and order.

Resolving the 'Eastern Question'

Inflated by his success, encouraged by his courtiers, and corrupted by power, the 'Autocrat of all the Russias' decided that the time had come to bring new lustre to the Russian Crown. All the great Tsars had added territory to the Russian Empire and Nicholas certainly considered himself to be a great Tsar. His eyes focused on the crumbling Ottoman Empire and Constantinople, which the Russians had coveted for a thousand years. Russia had already fought seven wars against Turkey, and it was not difficult to pick a quarrel. A Russian envoy was sent to Constantinople demanding certain concessions for the Orthodox Church at shrines in Jerusalem and recognition of Russia as the protector of the Sultan's Christian Slavs. At the same time Nicholas summoned the British Minister in St Petersburg and blandly suggested partitioning Turkey's European possessions between England and Russia.

Britain, suspicious of Russia's motives, doubted the sincerity of Nicholas's sanctimonious arguments, and she entered into an alliance with Napoleon III—the nephew of the man against whom Britain had fought so long and desperately when France had threatened the liberties of Europe. The British Ambassador in Constantinople was told to advise the Sultan to concede the Tsar's demand for Orthodox rights in Jerusalem but flatly to reject that of a Russian protectorate over Turkey's Christian subjects.

But Nicholas had gone too far to draw back. It was clear that Britain and France would side with Turkey, yet he found it difficult to believe they would actually go to war in defence of a ramshackle empire for which it was well known the Western Powers had little sympathy. Come what may he was determined to resolve the 'Eastern Question', as it was called in diplomatic circles. To the accompaniment of a good deal of talk about duty to God and Christianity, a Russian 'liberation' army crossed the Prut on 2 July 1853 and marched into the Danubian provinces of Moldavia and Wallachia which were then tributary to Turkey. The pretext was that Russia was holding this territory as a pledge for her just demands. The Turks demanded that the Russians retire and when no notice was taken they mobilized. Three months later they declared war on Russia.

When Nicholas rejected a joint ultimatum presented by Britain, France and Austria urging an immediate withdrawal from the Danubian principalities, war between the great powers was inevitable. Both sides had gone too far to give way without loss of prestige; an alliance was made between the Western Powers and Turkey and in March 1854 war was declared 'to protect Europe from the dominance of a power which violates treaties and defies the civilized world'.

Far from Vain

Little of the background was clear to the majority of people in Britain and France, and it is difficult to believe that people, in the

midst of an economic depression, shivering in an unusually cold
winter, and rioting because work on the land had stopped and with
it their miserable nine shillings a week, felt particularly enthusiastic about the prospect of war. But highly coloured descriptions
of the destruction of a Turkish fleet at Sinope had roused intense
feelings and in both countries the Press had been building up to a
crescendo of abuse in its references to Nicholas and praise for the
'brave but weak' Turks. Many of those whose dull little lives were
constrained by the field and factory, probably welcomed the excitement and quickening of national life which the crisis aroused.

No real consideration had been given to the problem of where
Russia would be brought to heel. When war was declared it appeared certain the lower Danube would be the main theatre of operations and the Caucasus the secondary theatre. In the event the
Black Sea was to become the seat of hostilities and the Crimean
Peninsula—which was to become the scene of the land fighting—
gave the war the name by which it is usually known. Except for
the naval base at Sebastopol, the Crimea had little strategic importance and if the Russians had abandoned it in 1854 the British
and French would have found it difficult to fight a land campaign.
But prestige demanded that the peninsula should be defended, and
with the enormous numerical superiority which the Russians enjoyed the fighting was bound to be hard and bitter. (In those days
soldiers fought standing shoulder to shoulder in ranks, exchanging fire with the enemy at point-blank range; fortunately weapons
were inaccurate and casualties light by modern standards.) For the
British army a long period of non-intervention in large-scale wars
and the effects upon Parliament of strong pacifist propaganda had
brought a decline in organization and administration. In consequence the British troops suffered extreme privations. The French,
who did not do so much fighting, were better prepared and better
organized for the campaign and they did not suffer to the same extent as the British. Wellington, it is said, once likened the organization of his army to a harness made of rope, and the French organization to one of leather. (The theory was that rope could be
knotted and it would still function, whereas repairs to a leather
harness were less simple.) In the Crimea what was left of Wellington's rope proved less durable than what the French had developed
from Napoleon's leather.

In its effects the war against Russia was far from being the
'vain' campaign which some early twentieth-century historians

dubbed it. In the field the British and French armies invariably defeated the Russians and inflicted on them such appalling casualties that they ceased to menace their neighbours for more than a generation. In Russia itself the internal economy suffered, and revolutionary propaganda which was finally to bring about the fall of the Tsarist Empire and the rise of the Soviet Union from its ruins was provided with fertile material. With the growth of the new Soviet Empire the advantages derived by Britain and France from their sacrifices in the Crimea may well seem nebulous. But it must be remembered that British soldiers were never called upon to fight in Europe between the fall of Sebastopol and the German invasion of Belgium in 1914, and in the same period Russia never attempted to interfere with French interests.

The War's Legacy and Innovations

The Crimean War is remembered principally by a cavalry charge and the heroism of a woman. Two films have been made of the famous Charge of the Light Brigade; none, surprisingly, of the Battle of the Alma when Her Majesty's Guards, in full regalia, marched magnificently into battle—in step and in perfect lines. The name of Lord Cardigan—the 'Noble Yachtsman' who led the charge and refused to share with his troops the rigours of camp life—has passed into the English language as an article of clothing. Florence Nightingale, the 'Lady with the Lamp' who devoted herself to the care of the sick and wounded, is credited with establishing the first system of hygienic hospital care for the wounded. The campaign showed how sea power could maintain comparatively small armies in the territory of a gigantic continental enemy and defeat every force that land power could bring against them, so long as their sea communications remained secure. This fact was not forgotten for a long time, but nowadays few people appreciate that much of the fighting of the campaign set the pattern of the wars which followed up to 1918. Balaclava, with its cavalry charges and 'thin red line', was but an echo from the wars of the past and it was soon superseded by the trench warfare which siege operations and high-velocity rifles imposed. Explosive shells had been in limited use up to 1854, but in the Crimea shell-fire was used to a degree unequalled in earlier wars.

This was also the beginning of the rifle era. At the Alma, Inkerman and the Tchernaya the rifle and bayonet were the decisive weapons and they remained so until the coming of the machine-gun, the tank and the aeroplane. Rifles had been used in the eighteenth century but the rate of fire was slow and they were so clumsy that with all its faults the old smooth-bore musket was considered to be the best all-round weapon. Between the close of the Napoleonic wars and the outbreak of the war with Russia, however, the rifle was being developed and from the 1830s onwards most European armies were being rearmed with one form or another of it. When tests showed that the Minié rifle with which the French army was being re-equipped was superior to the British Baker rifles which had been used by the British army in the Peninsula war, the British Government decided to set up a factory at Enfield to manufacture an 'Enfield' rifle of a design which incorporated the best features of the Minié and several other types then being made in Europe and America. The Crimean War caught the British army in the process of rearming, so that some units found themselves with the new Enfield, others with the Minié and a few with the Baker.

Among other innovations were the light military railway which linked the base at Balaclava with the front towards the end of the siege; the first electric telegraph to be used in war—enabling politicians to exercise a closer control over the generals than had ever been possible hitherto; the first professional war correspondent, W.H. Russell of *The Times;* and the first war photographer, Roger Fenton. This was the last important campaign in which the British soldier fought in full dress uniform, the last in which regiments carried their colours, and the last in which the infantry marched into battle behind their regimental bands. The battles of the Crimea are more than a hundred years away; we have seen two world wars and several sizeable 'little' wars since then, and presumably we ought to know something more of what sets cannon roaring and bombs falling. In England there are still plenty of public houses, terraces and cottages named after Alma, Balaclava and Inkerman to remind people of a war that was primarily an infantry war.

According to Ecclesiastes [the biblical book] 'The thing that hath been, it is that which shall be; and that which is done is that which shall be done: and there is no new thing under the sun.' The story of *The Vainglorious War* is full of the old lessons we live to forget and the traditions we shall remember. More than a century has elapsed since the events recaptured in the following pages. During that time there have been many cultural, technical and scientific advances. But nations' characters remain basically the same, and on this we should reflect.

13 Florence Nightingale Serves in the Crimean War: November 1854

The Founder of Modern Nursing

by Deborah Pulliam

England's Florence Nightingale (1820–1910) was the founder of modern nursing. One of the most prominent Englishwomen of the nineteenth century, Nightingale also was an influential figure in public health advocacy and hospital management. She produced numerous writings through which her commonsense, professional approach to the practice of medicine is evident.

Nightingale is best remembered for her service as a nurse during the Crimean War (1854–1856) in which England, France, and Turkey fought Russia. Until that time, nursing was a low-class, disreputable occupation often linked with coarseness and prostitution. In November 1854, Nightingale and thirty-eight nurses went to Scutari, Turkey, to tend to wounded British soldiers. She organized hospitals and arranged for improvements in food, water, and sanitation. Nightingale became known as "the Lady with the Lamp" for her nighttime ministrations by candlelight. In addition to comforting the sick, she kept records, collected data, and devised calculations for mortality rates among soldiers. Nightingale's reforms set new standards and transformed nursing into a respectable, organized profession.

In this article, freelance writer Deborah Pulliam traces the fifty-year career of Florence Nightingale. Writing after a visit to the Florence Nightingale Museum in London, Pulliam explains that the English nurse made many contributions to public health upon her return from the Crimea in 1856. She established a nursing school, penned tracts on principles of nursing and hospital management,

Deborah Pulliam, "Florence Nightingale: The Lady with the Lamp," *British Heritage Magazine*, January 1998. Copyright © 1998 by *British Heritage Magazine*. Reproduced by permission.

and contributed to the reform of the public health system in India.

Pulliam notes that in spite of her status as an international public health authority, Nightingale remained a private person who was uncomfortable in the limelight. She was, however, actively involved with the Nightingale Training School for Nurses at St. Thomas's Hospital, which she founded in 1860. Pulliam points out that despite advances in medicine since Nightingale's time, the ideas "the Lady with the Lamp" codified, and her emphasis on care and consideration for patients, remain a cornerstone of nursing.

F lorence Nightingale was distinctly not the romantic, retiring Victorian gentlewoman most of us imagine. She was a bright, tough, driven professional, a brilliant organizer and statistician, and one of the most influential women in 19th-century England.

Springboard for a Fifty-Year Career

The best-known aspect of her life—nursing wounded soldiers at Scutari Hospital in Turkey during the Crimean War—comprised, in fact, a very small part of her fifty-year career, but provided the springboard from which it all began.

Looking through a rough reproduction window at the London museum that bears her name is a little like peering over Nightingale's shoulder in the Crimea and confronting the intimate details of life there—including her hand-drawn plan of the nurses' quarters in the Barrack Hospital at Scutari, her personal seal and wax for letters, some of her books and her dispatch case, as well as an original letter written from the hospital and her famous lamp.

The museum's permanent exhibit documents not only the war years, but also follows Nightingale throughout her extraordinary but largely overlooked life. A brief introductory film emphasizes her wealthy Victorian upbringing and expectations of a brilliant social career.

In fact, Florence Nightingale accomplished so much during her full life that it is intriguing to wonder how she might be remembered had the public not become so fixated on the romantic image of her night-time rounds by candlelight at Scutari. This small museum highlights all of her many accomplishments: introducing sanitary science to nursing and the British Army; raising the image of the British soldier from a brawling lowlife to a heroic working man; transforming nursing from an occupation which previously had been considered fit only for prostitutes to a respectable profession; establishing a nursing school at St. Thomas's Hospital; laying out the principles of nursing in print in 1860; and revolutionizing the public health system of India without leaving England.

Shying Away from the Public

Ironically, during much of her long and accomplished life (she died in 1910, at the age of 90) the general public assumed she was already dead. Nightingale actually encouraged this misinformation. She returned from the Crimea under an assumed name and walked the last few miles to her parents' home from the train station. Uninterested in her celebrity status, she wanted only to continue her work in peace and quiet. She refused photographs and interviews, and avoided anything not directly related to her work for a Royal Commission investigating health in the British Army. Although she was undoubtedly the driving force behind the work, she almost never appeared in public.

Her thoughts and work were with the army. In a private note, written at the end of 1856, she wrote:

> Oh my poor men who endured so patiently. I feel I have been such a bad mother to you to come home and leave you lying in your Crimean grave. Seventy-three percent in eight regiments during six months from disease alone—who thinks of that now? But if I could carry any one point which would prevent any part of the recurrence of this our colossal calamity then I should have been true to the cause of those brave dead.

In the post-war period, Nightingale began studying new designs for modern hospitals all over Europe, in order to help the army reform its health and sanitary systems. In Paris she found a revolutionary design in which separate units, or pavilions, made up one large hospital. By making each pavilion a light and airy self-contained unit, the hospital minimized the spread of infections. She later succeeded in promoting this design in England.

Her research culminated in *Notes on Hospitals*, published in 1859, which combined two papers presented the year before at the Social Science Congress. Her words had a profound effect. She addressed every aspect of hospital management, from the purchase of iron bedsteads to replace the wooden ones, to switching to glass cups instead of tin.

An Authority on Hospital Management

The 108-page book went on into three editions and established Nightingale once more as an international authority. Her advice and approval were sought for hospitals all over Europe, from Holland to Portugal and even far-off India.

In particular, the governors of St. Thomas's Hospital in London consulted with her on a matter key to the hospital's future. The ancient hospital in Southwark was situated on land needed by railroads for a new line. The hospital's governors had to decide whether they should sell the entire property and build a new facility in a better location, or allow the railroad to buy only part of the land and rebuild the hospital on the remainder. Some governors felt the hospital should stay where it had been for hundreds of years, serving the same community.

When they asked Nightingale for her opinion, rather than simply accepting the notion that the hospital was in fact serving patients in the area, she drew up and analyzed statistics on the origin of St. Thomas's patients and proved that most did not come from the immediate neighbourhood as the governors had assumed.

She also compiled a convincing body of statistics to prove that moving the hospital to a healthier site would improve the patients' chances of recovery. After completing her analysis, in a telling dis-

Florence Nightingale (left) advocates clean conditions in hospitals where she provides aid for the wounded.

play of political acumen, she sent it not to the body of governors as a whole, but to one particular governor: the Prince Consort.

In the end, the governors decided to move St. Thomas's to its present location in Lambeth. At the time, Nightingale deemed the site to be unhealthy; nevertheless, the hospital was constructed with the pavilions she endorsed, and was finally completed in 1871. If you look carefully from Westminster Bridge, you can see the remaining pavilions wedged in between more contemporary parts of the hospital that have since engulfed the original. Ask for directions in the museum, and you can walk through the new parts of the hospital to Nightingale's original entrance hall.

Success piled on success. In 1860, after five years of gruelling work, she completed a voluminous report that resulted in the development of an Army Medical School in addition to greatly improved army barracks, hospitals, and living conditions for soldiers.

Also in 1860 she founded the Nightingale Training School for nurses at St. Thomas's Hospital. Far more than merely giving her name to the school, Nightingale personally advised on all matters of instruction, admissions supervision, and discipline. Her involvement extended beyond her professional duties; she often invited graduates to tea and kept in touch with them long after they had launched their careers.

Nightingale also published a 75-page booklet, *Notes on Nursing: What It Is, and What It Is Not.* A popular book, its initial reception still did not foretell of its lasting importance. The book is still in print today in a facsimilie of the first edition and in a reprint of the second enlarged edition. In fact, it is the best-selling item in the museum's small shop. "I think if you're only going to buy one thing from our shop, it's going to be *Notes on Nursing*," says Alex Attewell, curator of the museum.

While medical knowledge has significantly increased since Nightingale's time, her common sense and wisdom still forms a solid basis for caring for people. She believed, first and foremost, in hygiene (fresh air, cleanliness, clean water, proper drainage, and plenty of light), and constant consideration for the patient's feelings. In one particularly empathetic passage, she addresses the importance of a quiet environment:

> Unnecessary noise, or noise that creates an expectation in the mind, is that which hurts a patient. It is rarely the loudness of the noise, the effect upon the organ of the ear itself, which appears to

affect the sick. How well a patient will generally bear [for example] the putting up of a scaffolding close to the house, when he cannot bear the talking, still less the whispering, especially if it be a familiar voice, outside his door.

A Common-Sense Approach

Nightingale's common-sense approach to health is a main theme throughout the museum's exhibits. "We're interested in exploring what of her writing is still relevant today," Attewell says.

Because of her work on army medical reform, she was asked to contribute to a study of the problems of health in India. British troops on the subcontinent had the highest mortality rates of all—in 1859 the death rate was 69 per thousand, as opposed to 17 per thousand in England. Through statistics and endless study, (compiled, amazingly, without ever visiting India) she discovered what no one else had noticed: that the English way of life could simply not be transferred to a hot climate.

Her 23-page treatise on conditions in India (as compared with the government's 2,028 pages of small print) was printed at her own expense and sent to anyone with influence, including Queen Victoria. Once again, Nightingale revealed what no one even wanted to consider: that terrible living and working conditions were killing British troops as they had in the Crimea.

Yet again she emphasized that improving the health of British troops would require improving sanitary standards as a whole. For four years Nightingale worked daily on the meticulous paperwork and statistics required to reform life in India. Her influence went beyond paperwork. Newly assigned viceroys to India visited her home for briefings before setting out for their new post.

In 1896, Nightingale "retired to her bed," but, far from slowing down, she continued working on home health visiting, as the English call public health. "Her writing is extraordinarily relevant to today's health visiting," Attewell says.

In an attempt to find out just how pertinent her writing is to the health profession today, the museum sent out questionnaires to 700 public health supervisors around the country. More than half came back almost immediately. "Usually you'd think a 10 per cent response would be good," Attewell says. "I think the interest we've got in the questionnaire shows there's still extraordinary interest in her writing." Yet more evidence of the timeless value in the work and wisdom of this remarkable woman.

14 Darwin Presents the Theory of Evolution: November 24, 1859

The Darwinian Revolution Had Profound Effects

by Michael Ruse

On November 24, 1859, British biologist Charles Darwin published *On the Origin of Species.* This important work, in which Darwin presented his theory of evolution by natural selection, was controversial from the start, as it pitted the concept of evolution by biological adaptation of natural selection against religious ideas about divine creation and existing scientific ideas about permanence in nature.

Darwin's theory has often been misunderstood. The concept of evolution had been a point of discussion in scientific circles before the publication of Darwin's work. What Darwin achieved was an explanation for evolution; that is, he theorized that it occurred by means of natural selection. Darwin derived his conclusions through his observations of animal life on the Galapagos Islands while voyaging on the HMS *Beagle.* In his theory, Darwin suggested that in any given environment, species struggle to adapt. Those populations that survive are the most suitable for that particular type of environment. Therefore, each species must be capable of variation should more adaptability be required over time.

In the following selection, Michael Ruse probes the scientific basis of Darwin's theory of evolution. He also evaluates the contributions and understanding of other key scientists, as well as the influence of Darwin on scientific thought. In addition, Ruse assesses the impact of *On the Origin of Species* on philosophy and religion. The author concludes by noting that the Darwinian revolution in thought had numerous aspects, numerous causes, and numerous effects.

Michael Ruse, an author of several books, is professor of philosophy at Florida State University. He specializes in the philosophy of biology and has devoted much of his research to Darwinism.

T he bare bones of the tale can be quickly reviewed. In Britain in 1830 there was division of opinion on the organic origins question, but virtually no one was an evolutionist. Some favored an unknown but essentially law-bound originating mechanism; others supported miracles. In 1844, when [Robert] Chambers published his *Vestiges*, almost no member of the professional scientific community accepted its central message; but in 1859, when [Charles] Darwin published the *Origin*, scientists concerned with the origins of organisms were rapidly converted to evolutionism. Yet even Darwin had only limited success, for many refused to accept fully his mechanism for evolutionary change, natural selection. All the threads around which our narrative has been structured throw light on this course of events.

Scientific Facts Help Evolutionists

First, matters could be considered at the purely *scientific* level. Many facts that were inexplicable if not downright anomalous from a nonevolutionary viewpoint fitted into place for an evolutionist. And knowledge of such facts grew during our half-century. [Sir Charles] Lyell brought systematic order to these problems, but he did so despite himself, to highlight the difficulties for a nonevolutionist. Perhaps the most dramatic new knowledge was the distribution of finches and tortoises on the Galápagos Islands, as revealed by Darwin himself. For any nonevolutionist this caused problems. One could certainly suppose that God put different finches on different islands, but this seems pointless at best, if not a direct violation of God's good sense. And Lyell, supposing laws but not evolution, was in no better position. If the finches came from elsewhere, how and why were they distributed as they were? If the finches started life on the various islands, how could this happen except by a process suspiciously like evolution?

Perhaps no facts were quite as dramatic as those of geographical distribution, but other areas did not comfort nonevolutionists. In 1830 people read the fossil record more or less as they pleased. . . . Hence evolutionism came to appear more reasonable, especially an evolution like Darwin's, with no inevitable progression. The gaps in the record started to close, though the record was always sufficiently incomplete to permit causal interpretations other than selection. Much the same is true of morphology. It was clear that homologies needed explanation, and though [Sir Richard] Owen's archetype theory sufficed for a while, it had serious scientific flaws quite aside from the more philosophical objections opposed to the whole notion of archetypes.

Science also shows why people rejected *Vestiges*, though reactions to it certainly were not exclusively scientific. *Vestiges* was saddled with all kinds of untenable assumptions, like spontaneous generation; and the positive evidence was not as strong for Chambers as for Darwin. Chambers's main scientific argument came from the fossil record, and in 1844 there was much less reason to see it as evolutionary than there was in the 1860s. Chambers, and [Jean Baptiste] Lamarck for that matter, made no real attempt to solve one of the major puzzles—the origins of species as opposed to the origins of organisms. For Lamarck species were an embarrassment; for Chambers species were an accidental by-product of evolution. But for Darwin species were a natural consequence of basic principles.

Finally, science throws light on reactions to Darwin's doctrines aside from his general evolutionism. There were good scientific reasons to doubt that selection working on the smallest of variations could be effective enough to cause evolution. Darwin's speculations on the nature and causes of heredity and variation left much to be desired; and physics apparently showed that the time available for evolution was far too short for such a leisurely mechanism as selection. Science also shows the rationale of those who went furthest with Darwin. . . .

The Role of Philosophy

Philosophy yields much the same tale as science. Throughout our period scientists felt a metascientific urge to explain through law, bound up with a general belief that science ought, as much as possible, to imitate Newtonian physics (particularly the Newtonian astronomy of the 1830s). For all their subtlety, the nonevolutionists fell short of their own ideals, in others' eyes if not in their own. [W.] Whewell and [A.] Sedgwick divorced the organic origins question from science—to less conservative scientists a cure somewhat worse than the disease—and people like Lyell and [Sir

John Frederick William] Herschel knew well that their nonevolutionism came dangerously close to violating their empiricist *verae causae* principles. A major motive behind Chambers's work clearly was his desire to explain through law, and the same holds for Darwin and for those who responded favorably to his writings. Good Newtonian science requires law, and in the end only evolution could provide it.

Here in the philosophical realm, perhaps more than anywhere, we can see the advantage Darwin had over Chambers and understand why Darwin succeeded and Chambers did not. For all his talk of being Newtonian, Chambers really made no attempt to provide a *vera causa* for evolution, and his critics quickly noted this. Darwin certainly did not satisfy everyone, friend or foe, with his mechanism of natural selection; but in the *Origin* he made a systematic attempt to conform to criteria of scientific excellence, and the powerful effect of the *Origin* in large part sprang from this care. However, for empiricists like [J.] Huxley, employing an analogical *vera causa* concept, Darwin's failure to demonstrate that selection did lead to species change left the mechanism unproved. . . .

Religion and Evolutionism

Concerning *religion*, the major question might be not how religion helped the cause of evolutionism, but why it failed to suppress it. Even at the beginning of our period people had become accustomed to modifying their religion to accommodate the advances of science; so, while evolutionism may have been a serious problem, the threat was not really new. In our half-century we see religion continuing a retreat that had started long before. Yet religion was still a major force behind the nonevolutionary positions formulated in the 1830s. Religious people were terrified by the threat evolution posed to the special status of man, and both those for law and those for miracle cared desperately that full place be left for God's designing powers. Religion was also a major element in the reaction against Chambers. With good reason, he was considered to undermine the dignity of man and to leave no room for God's design. And much the same points came up again after the *Origin*. For various reasons these points were becoming less powerful—man's special status was coming under fire for reasons outside Darwinism, and Darwin had made some attempt to come to grips with adaptation—but many still felt the need to soften Darwin's speculations with elements of religion.

However, the Darwinian Revolution was not exclusively a war of science against religion, even if the two are considered distinct. In certain ways, unintentional and intentional, religion aided the coming of evolutionism—even Darwin's version. Unintentionally, evolutionism was undoubtedly helped by those like [Jean Louis Rodolphe] Agassiz and Miller, who made so much of the progressive nature of the fossil record, and the same holds true of the morphological version of the argument from design. By stressing homologies, such natural theologians were preparing the way for an evolutionary interpretation. Even Whewell, though he was never an evolutionist, helped spread the idea of law when he adopted Owen's archetypes and emphasized the morphological version of the design argument. And the utilitarian design argument, focusing upon and highlighting the importance of adaptation, contributed to Darwin's discovery of natural selection. Intentionally, evolutionism was helped by those who saw the highest mark of God's power as his ability to work through unbroken law—who saw God as a super leader of industry. This approach to religion spurred Chambers, Baden Powell, and many others. And somewhere on the borderline between intentionality and unintentionality we must find a place for Lyellian geology. Lyell found his approach to geology attractive because it alone satisfied his deistic concept of theology. But Lyellian geology, molded as it was by religion, was probably the major influence in bringing about Darwinian evolutionism, though the parent was not altogether happy with the child. Thus it is clear that evolutionism, and even selection, came because of religion as well as despite it.

Social and Political Factors

Finally, we must consider *social and political* factors. Between 1830 and 1875 we see an evolution of British society, and in particular British scientific society. In the 1830s science as a profession (particularly biology, geology, and the like) was just beginning, and because of the peculiarities of British higher education there were strong links between science and organized religion. The next forty to fifty years saw those links weaken and break, until it was possible for someone without independent means both to become a professional biologist or geologist and to owe nothing whatever to the church. Evolutionism, particularly Darwinian evolutionism, gained by this, though the opportunity had to be used. Darwin succeeded where Chambers failed because Darwin had earned respect as a scientist and because he had built up a group prepared to battle for his ideas. But given that the Church of England was an integral part of the establishment, the Darwinian Revolution also reflected the way power and authority were being loosed from the hold of an exclusive minority and shared by a wider middle class. In this most important change in Victorian Britain, the Darwinian Revolution was part cause and part effect.

I have taken up the various threads separately. They have crossed, intertwined, and run together, and often when advance in one area seemed blocked another came into play. When Darwin was faulted on religious grounds because he had paid too little attention to God as designer, he replied on philosophical grounds that such an explanation is neither required nor allowed in the physical sciences and therefore ought not be required or allowed in the biological sciences. Similarly, the science/religion compromise formulated by Sedgwick and Whewell, depending centrally on man's recent origin, was badly jolted by scientific discoveries about man's long history.

But separately or together, the various elements of our story point to one important conclusion, hinted at the beginning of this book: The Darwinian Revolution cannot be considered a single thing. It had different sides, different causes, and different effects. Often it is portrayed as a triumph of science over religion; but, though there is some truth to this idea, as a total assessment of the Darwinian Revolution it is far from adequate. The supposed triumph of science over religion was questionable, more was involved than science and religion, and in some respects religion helped the cause of science. It probably is a mistake to say that in the coming of evolutionism certain things were essential, whereas others were not. It makes little sense to compare the relative merits of, say, [H.W.] Bates's work on mimicry with Huxley's writing of supportive referee's reports for all who favored evolutionism. I would feel very uncomfortable with an analysis of the Darwinian Revolution that belittled these points to concentrate solely on the "real" issues, such as man's place in the natural scheme of things. In its way the Darwinian Revolution was one of the most significant movements in man's history. That it had many sides, intellectual and otherwise, should be no surprise. Indeed, we should have expected this.

14 Darwin Presents the Theory of Evolution: November 24, 1859

The Theory of Evolution Withstands Objections

by Charles Darwin

On the Origin of Species, published by Charles Darwin in 1859, is the shortened title of the biologist's major work. The full title, *On the Origin of Species by Means of Natural Selection, or the Preservation of Favoured Races in the Struggle for Life*, indicates the naturalistic mechanism behind Darwin's theory of evolution. Indeed, natural selection maintains that species with the ability to adapt in the struggle for existence are the ones that will survive and reproduce.

Darwin (1809–1882) served as a naturalist aboard the HMS *Beagle* from 1831 to 1836. While traveling on this British science expedition, Darwin made a shrewd observation: The fossils of extinct species in South America were similar in type to modern species, both in South America and on the Galápagos Islands in the Pacific Ocean. Darwin took notes and collected specimens throughout the voyage and ultimately came to the conclusion that evolution occurred very gradually by means of natural selection.

In the following excerpt from *On the Origin of Species*, Darwin summarizes his theory. He also acknowledges the objections and difficulties in the theory. He addresses the initial sterilization among cross-fertilized species, the matter of geographical distribution, and

Charles Darwin, *On the Origin of Species by Means of Natural Selection, or the Preservation of Favoured Races in the Struggle for Life*. New York: Modern Library, 1936.

the problem of "missing" links. Darwin realizes that the latter is a key criticism of the evolution theory. If evolution is gradual, then there must be evidence of evolutionary gradations in species that ultimately connect long-extinct fossils to the species of the modern world. Darwin concludes by supposing that the fossil record is imperfect and that those specimens that have been collected are but a sample of the number of species in existence over time.

T hat many and serious objections may be advanced against the theory of descent with modification through variation and natural selection, I do not deny. I have endeavoured to give to them their full force. Nothing at first can appear more difficult to believe than that the more complex organs and instincts have been perfected, not by means superior to, though analogous with, human reason, but by the accumulation of innumerable slight variations, each good for the individual possessor. Nevertheless, this difficulty, though appearing to our imagination insuperably great, cannot be considered real if we admit the following propositions, namely, that all parts of the organisation and instincts offer, at least, individual differences—that there is a struggle for existence leading to the preservation of profitable deviations of structure or instinct—and, lastly, that gradations in the state of perfection of each organ may have existed, each good of its kind. The truth of these propositions cannot, I think, be disputed.

Difficulties in the Theory

It is, no doubt, extremely difficult even to conjecture by what gradations many structures have been perfected, more especially amongst broken and failing groups of organic beings, which have suffered much extinction, but we see so many strange gradations in nature, that we ought to be extremely cautious in saying that any organ or instinct, or any whole structure, could not have arrived at its present state by many graduated steps. There are, it must be admitted, cases of special difficulty opposed to the theory of natural selection; and one of the most curious of these is the existence in the same community of two or three defined castes of workers or sterile female ants; but I have attempted to show how these difficulties can be mastered.

With respect to the almost universal sterility of species when first crossed, which forms so remarkable a contrast with the almost universal fertility of varieties when crossed, . . . which seem to me conclusively to show that this sterility is no more a special endowment than is the incapacity of two distinct kinds of trees to be grafted together; but that it is incidental on differences confined to the reproductive systems of the intercrossed species. We see the truth of this conclusion in the vast difference in the results of crossing the same two species reciprocally,—that is, when one species is first used as the father and then as the mother. Analogy from the consideration of dimorphic and trimorphic plants clearly leads to the same conclusion, for when the forms are illegitimately united, they yield few or no seed, and their offspring are more or less sterile; and these forms belong to the same undoubted species, and differ from each other in no respect except in their reproductive organs and functions. . . .

Charles Darwin

Turning to geographical distribution, the difficulties encountered on the theory of descent with modification are serious enough. All the individuals of the same species, and all the species of the same genus, or even higher group, are descended from common parents; and therefore, in however distant and isolated parts of the world they may now be found, they must in the course of successive generations have travelled from some one point to all the others. We are often wholly unable even to conjecture how this could have been effected. Yet, as we have reason to believe that some species have retained the same specific form for very long periods of time, immensely long as measured by years, too much stress ought not to be laid on the occasional wide diffusion of the same species; for during very long periods there will always have been a good chance for wide migration by many means. A broken or interrupted range may often be accounted for by the extinction of the species in the intermediate regions. It cannot be denied that we are as yet very ignorant as to the full extent of the various climatal and geographical changes which have affected the earth during modern periods; and such changes will often have facilitated migration. As an example, I have attempted to show how potent has been the influence of the Glacial period on the distribution of the same and of allied species throughout the world. We are as yet profoundly ignorant of the many occasional means of transport. With respect to distinct species of the same genus inhabiting distant and isolated regions, as the process of modification has necessarily been slow, all the means of migration will have been possible during a very long period; and consequently the difficulty of the wide diffusion of the species of the same genus is in some degree lessened.

Questions About Links

As according to the theory of natural selection an interminable number of intermediate forms must have existed, linking together all the species in each group by gradations as fine as are our existing varieties, it may be asked. Why do we not see these linking forms all around us? Why are not all organic beings blended together in an inextricable chaos? With respect to existing forms, we should remember that we have no right to expect (excepting in rare cases) to discover *directly* connecting links between them, but only between each and some extinct and supplanted form. Even on a wide area, which has during a long period remained continuous, and of which the climatic and other conditions of life change insensibly in proceeding from a district occupied by one species into another district occupied by a closely allied species, we have no just right to expect often to find intermediate varieties in the intermediate zones. For we have reason to believe that only a few species of a genus ever undergo change; the other species becoming utterly extinct and leaving no modified progeny. Of the species which do change, only a few within the same country change at the same time; and all modifications are slowly effected. I have also shown that the intermediate varieties which probably at first existed in the intermediate zones, would be liable to be supplanted by the allied forms on either hand; for the latter, from existing in greater numbers, would generally be modified and improved at a quicker rate than the intermediate varieties, which existed in lesser numbers; so that the intermediate varieties would, in the long run, be supplanted and exterminated.

On this doctrine of the extermination of an infinitude of connecting links, between the living and extinct inhabitants of the world, and at each successive period between the extinct and still older species, why is not every geological formation charged with such links? Why does not every collection of fossil remains afford plain evidence of the gradation and mutation of the forms of life? Although geological research has undoubtedly revealed the former existence of many links, bringing numerous forms of life much closer together, it does not yield the infinitely many fine gradations between past and present species required on the theory; and this is the most obvious of the many objections which may be urged against it. Why, again, do whole groups of allied species appear, though this appearance is often false, to have come in suddenly on the successive geological stages? Although we now know that organic beings appeared on this globe, at a period incalculably remote, long before the lowest bed of the Cambrian system was deposited, why do we not find beneath this system great piles of strata stored with the remains of the progenitors of the Cambrian fossils? For on the theory, such strata must somewhere have been deposited at these ancient and utterly unknown epochs of the world's history.

CHRONOLOGY

1840

June: The British send warships to China and the First Opium War between Great Britain and China begins.

1842

The Webster-Ashburton Treaty between the United States and Great Britain defines the U.S.-Canadian border.
August 29: The First Opium War ends; the Treaty of Nanking, in which China cedes Hong Kong to England, is signed.

1843

The SS *Great Britain* is the first propeller-driven, iron-hulled steamship to cross the Atlantic Ocean; Charles Dickens publishes *A Christmas Carol.*

1844

May 24: Samuel F.B. Morse's telegraph is successful. The first message is transmitted forty miles, from Washington to Baltimore.
October 15: German philosopher Friedrich Nietszche, who challenged traditional Christian morality by claiming that "God is dead" and man is at an existential turning point, is born.

1845

June: A potato blight strikes Ireland. Ruined crops and rising food prices devastate the country for several years.
December 29: Texas, a Mexican province that declared independence in 1836, is annexed to the United States.

1846

As a result of the Irish potato famine, the British Parliament repeals the Corn Laws. The end of the protectionist laws, which had kept the price of corn artificially high, further opened Great Britain to free trade.
May 13: The U.S.-Mexican War begins.

September 10: American inventor Elias Howe patents the sewing machine.

October 16: The first public demonstration of ether as a surgical anesthetic proves successful.

1848

January: The *Communist Manifesto*, by Karl Marx and Friedrich Engels, is published as a pamphlet.

January 24: Gold is discovered at Sutter's Mill in California, inaugurating the gold rush period during which Americans flocked to California in hopes of striking it rich.

February 2: The Treaty of Guadalupe between the United States and Mexico is signed. Mexico is to cede more than half its territory to the United States.

February 22–24: A revolution in Paris forces the abdication of King Louis-Philippe. In the months that follow, revolutions occur in Austria, Germany, Italy, and Poland.

May 30: The Treaty of Guadalupe ending the U.S.-Mexican War is ratified.

July 19–20: The first woman's rights convention meets in Seneca Falls, New York, marking the birth of an organized women's movement.

1849

Victor Emmanuel II becomes king of Savoy, Piedmont, and Sardinia; he will rule this region until the Italian Unification of 1861, when he becomes king of Italy. (1878).

1850

The Taiping Rebellion begins in China. The leader of the rebellion, an adherent of a political creed influenced by Christianity, seeks to establish a new dynasty. Although "Taiping" means "Great Peace," this is a very bloody conflict. German chemist Robert Bunsen perfects the gas-based Bunsen burner.

January 29: U.S. senator Henry Clay proposes the Compromise of 1850. Eventually passed, the congressional act puts the Fugitive Slave Law, which entitled slave owners to pursue and retrieve escaped slaves, into effect.

1851

Herman Melville publishes *Moby Dick;* the *New York Times* begins circulation.

May 1–October 15: The Great Exhibition, an international display of manufactured goods, takes place in Hyde Park, London.

December: Louis, nephew of Napoléon, is elected president of France and later becomes Emperor Napoléon III.

1852

March 20: *Uncle Tom's Cabin*, an antislavery novel by Harriet Beecher Stowe, is published in book form.

1853

July 14: Commodore Matthew Perry establishes a diplomatic relationship with Japan, ending centuries of Japan's self-imposed isolation.

1854

Henry David Thoreau's *Walden* is published. An account of Thoreau's stay in a cabin on Walden Pond in Concord, Massachusetts, the book combined nature writing and social criticism.

March 28: The Crimean War, in which Russia fought the Ottoman Empire (Turkey), France, and Great Britain, begins.

November: Florence Nightingale, pioneer of modern nursing, travels with thirty-eight nurses to the Crimea to tend to the war wounded.

1855

September: The Russian fortress of Sevastopol falls, a decisive turning point in the Crimean War.

1856

March 30: The Treaty of Paris ends the Crimean War.

October 8: The Second Opium War between China and Great Britain begins. France enters on the side of the British.

1857

Guiseppe Garibaldi, a nationalist, forms the Italian National Association for the Unification of Italy; the Sepoy Mutiny, or First

War of Indian Independence, erupts in Northern India, marking the first united rebellion against British colonial rule.

1858
As a result of the Sepoy Mutiny, the British Parliament takes control of India from the British East India Company, longtime administrators that provided the model for Britain's own civil service.

1859
The War of the National Unification of Italy, which will last until 1861, begins.
April 25: Construction begins on the Suez Canal, opening a vital sea route between the Mediterranean and Red seas.
November 24: Charles Darwin presents his theory of evolution by natural selection in *On the Origin of Species.*

1860
Belgian-born engineer and inventor J.J.E. Lenoir patents the first internal combustion engine, which later becomes the central component of automobiles.
October: The Second Opium War comes to an end; China is defeated.

FOR FURTHER RESEARCH

Books

Jeffrey Auerbach, *The Great Exhibition of 1851*. New Haven, CT: Yale University Press, 1999.

Shlomo Barer, *Doctors of Revolution: 19th-Century Thinkers Who Changed the World*. New York: Thames & Hudson, 2000.

A.J. Barker, *The Vainglorious War: 1854–1856*. London: Weidenfeld and Nicolson, 1970.

Charles Darwin, *On the Origin of Species by Means of Natural Selection, or the Preservation of Favoured Races in the Struggle for Life*. 1859. Reprint, New York: Modern Library, 1936.

Daniel C. Dennett, *Darwin's Dangerous Idea: Evolution and the Meanings of Life*. New York: Simon & Schuster, 1996.

Ellen C. DuBois, ed., *The Elizabeth Cady Stanton–Susan B. Anthony Reader: Speeches, Writing, Correspondence*. Boston: Northeastern University Press, 1992.

Terry Eagleton, *Marx*. Great Philosophers Series. New York: Routledge, 1999.

John S. Eisenhower, *So Far from God: The U.S. War with Mexico, 1846–1848*. Norman: University of Oklahoma Press, 2000.

John Erichsen, *The Science and Art of Surgery*. Ed. John H. Brinton. Philadelphia: Blanchard and Lea, 1854.

Peter Ward Fay, *The Opium War, 1840–1842: Barbarians in the Celestial Empire in the Early Part of the Nineteenth Century*. Chapel Hill: University of North Carolina Press, 1997.

Julie M. Fenster, *Ether Day: The Strange Tale of America's Greatest Medical Discovery and the Haunted Men Who Made It*. New York: HarperCollins, 2002.

Eleanor Flexner, *Century of Struggle: The Woman's Rights Movement in the United States.* Cambridge, MA: Belknap, 1959.

Murray Forsyth, H.M.A. Keens-Soper, and Maurice Keens-Soper, eds., *The Political Classics: Hamilton to Mill.* New York: Oxford University Press, 1994.

Sue M. Goldie, *Florence Nightingale: Letters from the Crimea, 1854–1856.* New York: St. Martin's, 1997.

Miriam Gurko, *The Ladies of Seneca Falls: The Birth of the Woman's Rights Movement.* New York: Knopf, 1976.

Ann Hagedorn, *Beyond the River: A True Story of the Underground Railroad.* New York: Simon & Schuster, 2003.

William Travis Hanes and Frank Sanello, *Opium Wars: The Addiction of One Empire and Corruption of Another.* Naperville, IL: Sourcebooks, 2002.

Michael Hanne, *The Power of the Story: Fiction and Political Change.* Providence, RI: Berghahn, 1994.

Wilhelm Heine, *With Perry to Japan: A Memoir.* Trans. Frederic Trautmann. Honolulu: University of Hawaii Press, 1990.

Colleen A. Hobbs, *Florence Nightingale.* New York: Twayne, 1997.

Hermione Hobhouse, *Crystal Palace and the Great Exhibition: Art, Science, and Productive Industry. A History of the Royal Commission for the Exhibition of 1851.* New York: Continuum, 2002.

Eric J. Hobsbawm, *The Age of the Revolution: 1789–1848.* San Francisco: David McKay, 1996.

Marius B. Jansen, *The Making of Modern Japan.* Cambridge, MA: Belknap, 2000.

Robert W. Johannsen, *To the Halls of the Montezumas: The Mexican War and the American Imagination.* New York: Oxford University Press, 1985.

Noel Kissane, ed., *Irish Famine: A Documentary History.* Syracuse, NY: Syracuse University Press, 1996.

P.C. Kuo, ed., *A Critical Study of the First Anglo-Chinese War: With Documents.* Shanghai, China: Commercial, 1935.

Mason I. Lowance, Ellen E. Westbrook, and R.C. DeProspo, eds., *Stowe Debate: Rhetorical Strategies in* Uncle Tom's Cabin. Amherst: University of Massachusetts Press, 1994.

Karl Marx and Friederick Engels, *Manifesto of the Communist Party.* Ed. and annotated by Friederick Engels. 1888. Reprint, New York: International, 1996.

James L. McClain, *A Modern History: Japan.* New York: W.W. Norton, 2002.

Eric L. McKitrick, ed., *Slavery Defended: The Views of the Old South.* Englewood Cliffs, NJ: Prentice-Hall, 1963.

Samuel F.B. Morse, *Samuel F.B. Morse: His Letters and Journals.* Ed. and supplemented by Edward Lind Morse. Vol. 2. Boston and New York: Houghton Mifflin, 1914.

Margaret M. Mulrooney, ed., *Fleeing the Famine: North America and Irish Refugees, 1845–1851.* Westport, CT: Greenwood, 2003.

Florence Nightingale, *Notes on Nursing: What It Is, What It Is Not.* 1860. Reprint, New York: Barnes & Noble, 2003.

Cormac O'Grada, *Black '47 and Beyond: The Great Irish Famine in History, Economy, and Memory.* Princeton, NJ: Princeton University Press, 1999.

Beverly Wilson Palmer, Carol Faulkner, and Holly Byers Ochoa, eds., *Selected Letters of Lucretia Coffin Mott.* Champaign: University of Illinois Press, 2001.

Martin S. Pernick, *A Calculus of Suffering: Pain, Professionalism, and Anesthesia in Nineteenth-Century America.* New York: Columbia University Press, 1985.

Matthew Calbraith Perry, *The Japan Expedition, 1852–1854: The Personal Journal of Commodore Matthew C. Perry.* Washington, DC: Smithsonian Institution, 1968.

James K. Polk, *The Diary of James K. Polk During His Presidency, 1845 to 1849.* 1910. Reprint, New York: Kraus, 1970.

Roy Porter, *Blood and Guts: A Short History of Medicine.* New York: W.W. Norton, 2003.

Roger Price, *The Revolutions of 1848.* Atlantic Highlands, NJ: Humanities, 1989.

Samuel I. Prime, *The Life of Samuel F.B. Morse.* New York: D. Appleton, 1875.

John O'Beirne Ranelagh, *A Short History of Ireland.* Cambridge, England: Cambridge University Press, 1983.

Thomas Richards, *The Commodity Culture of Victorian England: Advertising and Spectacle, 1851–1914.* Stanford, CA: Stanford University Press, 1990.

Trevor Royle, *Crimea: The Great Crimean War, 1854–1856.* New York: St. Martin's, 2000.

Michael Ruse, *The Darwinian Revolution: Science Red in Tooth and Claw.* 2nd ed. Chicago: University of Chicago Press, 1999.

William Howard Russell, *The British Expedition to the Crimea.* London: Routledge, 1858.

Paul W. Schroeder, *Austria, Great Britain, and the Crimean War: The Destruction of the European Concert.* Ithaca, NY: Cornell University Press, 1972.

F.B. Smith, *Florence Nightingale: Reputation and Power.* New York: St. Martin's, 1982.

Jonathan Sperber, *The European Revolutions, 1848–1851.* Cambridge, UK: Cambridge University Press, 1994.

Peter N. Stearns, *1848: The Revolutionary Tide in Europe.* New York: W.W. Norton, 1974.

Anders Stephanson, *Manifest Destiny: American Expansionism and the Empire of Right.* New York: Farrar, Straus, and Giroux, 1995.

Harriet Beecher Stowe, *Uncle Tom's Cabin.* 1851–1852. Reprint, Columbus, OH: Merrill, 1969.

Robert L. Thompson, *Wiring a Continent: The History of the Tele-*

graph Industry in the United States, 1832–1866. Princeton, NJ: Princeton University Press, 1947.

Robert C. Tucker and David P. McLellan, eds., *The Marx-Engels Reader.* 2nd ed. New York: W.W. Norton, 1978.

Arthur D. Waley, *The Opium War Through Chinese Eyes.* Stanford, CA: Stanford University Press, 1990.

Arthur Walworth, *Black Ships off Japan: The Story of Commodore Perry's Expedition.* Hamden, CT: Archon, 1966.

Thomas Woodward, *Doubts About Darwin: A History of Intelligent Design.* Grand Rapids, MI: Baker, 2003.

Daniel A.Wren and Ronald G. Greenwood, *Management Innovators: The People and Ideas That Have Shaped Modern Business.* New York: Oxford University Press, 1998.

Web Sites

Digital History, www.digitalhistory.uh.edu. A comprehensive resource, this exceptionally thorough collaboration of the University of Houston, the Chicago Historical Society, and the U.S. Department of the Interior covers U.S. history since its origins. In addition to interactive time lines, the site offers an encyclopedia, biographies, and links to archives of primary source documents.

Timelines of History, http://timelines.ws. This online resource contains detailed time lines of history from the ancient world to the present, searchable by time period—century, decade, year—or by subject categories such as disasters, technology, and artists.

World Civilizations: World Timeline, www.wwnorton.com/college/history/worldciv/referenc/wrldtime.htm. A collection of historical time lines, this site covers all civilizations in world history. A multimedia resource offers primary sources, pictures, maps, and information on specific subjects.

INDEX